Text Copyright © 2017 Keren Shamay

First Published by Shamay Holdings , LLC

All Rights Reserved. No part of this book may be reproduced in any form or by any electronic means including information storage and retrieval systems without the written permission of the copyright holder

ISBN 978-0692980934

For Sharon and Estella. Thank you for all the support.

Table of Contents

Table of Contents 3

Index 4

What are Vibrations? 8

Energy Work Throughout History 21

Accountability Matters 39

Chakras & Kundalini 46

Always Protect Yourself 55

You Can't Think Through It 73

Personal Accountability 82

YOU Caused It 100

Energy Blocks 108

Your Experience Is Your Own 125

All Modalities Work 136

References 145

Index

Ascension Journey – The Ascension journey references the process of raising your personal vibration. It is called a journey because there is no end. Once you start on this path, it continues to evolve.

Chakras – The energy centers throughout the human body. There are seven primary chakras: Root, Sacral, Solar Plexus, Heart, Throat, Third Eye and Crown. Chakras are believed to be part of the energy body, not the physical solid corporeal body. As such, they are the meeting points of the non-physical pathways through which life energy (also known as Chi) moves. Although these 7 are the most commonly known, the human body has hundreds of chakras throughout.

Downloads – The way in which higher intelligence enters our energy body and our conscious mind. This is always how our own energy is transmuted and raised. The downloads are believed to come from the Universe, or God depending on your belief system, and provide us with information which we need in order to reach greater levels of awareness.

Energetically Open – A way of describing someone who has connected to their intuition, or inner knowing, and has tapped into that knowledge. They may be completely unaware of this fact, but they still experience the things that come with being aware of energy.

Grounding – Also known as to ground. This is the person who acts as an anchor for those working with energy. This ensures that they can return to their body if they happen to leave during their work.

Guardians – These are beings which are created by the people they are guarding. They are internal projections of a defense system. These beings are good for the person they are protecting, but harmful for anyone who tries to access that individual psychically. They will allow someone entry if the person they are guarding gives explicit permission. They can cause physical and psychic damage to anyone who attempts to enter without permission. Physical symptoms can be pain, shaking, light headedness, etc. Psychic damage could include thoughts that are out of the normal range. They can also include emotional swings far greater than normally experienced.

Guides – These are energetic beings who have taken on the role of helping people navigate life with ease, by giving advice and options when asked. Their entire goal is to support you along your journey.

Healing Circle – Also known as Circle. When a few practitioners get together in order to focus healing energy toward one person, event, or place.

Higher Self – This is your highest energetic expression. You can think of this as the ultimate expression of your soul. Your higher self is the one ultimately in charge of the life path you have taken. It can give permission, or withhold it, based on the life path you have chosen regardless of your conscious self. Your higher self is ultimately concerned with your spiritual evolution.

Hitchhikers – These are spirits and / or ghosts who attach themselves to people in order to "leech" off their personal life energy. They are usually found in places with lots of lights, loud noises, and people who are experiencing emotional highs and lows. These places can include bars, casinos, McDonalds, or anywhere you find children and loud noises.

Kundalini – Also known as the sleeping serpent. This term refers to the dormant spiritual self which, when awakened, causes enlightenment. Many people try to activate their kundalini in order to gain psychic powers.

Light – This term generally refers to the light of God or the Universe. This can be accessed by connecting to the spirituality experienced during prayer. Generally when people are connecting to the Light and bringing it in, they are pulling the energy of love into their bodies.

Light Worker – Refers to someone who uses their abilities to connect with the Light to help others in this lifetime. Someone who is connected to their healing abilities and internal guidance. Psychics, healers, channels, etc. fall under this umbrella.

Medicine People – Colloquial term describing people from indigenous cultures and tribes who were taught healing arts by the elders of those tribes. They are tribal healers and use earth medicines which includes energy and plants. These people are much more connected to the earth and the natural healing arts than western populations.

Mindfulness – Being aware of your actions, and how you affect your own experience, and that of others.

Space Clearing – The use of energy and other items like the burning of sage or the sound of bells in order to clear the energy of a room. Scientifically, when a negative event happens, positive ions are released into that space and will stay until they are cleared. Space clearing involves creating enough negative ions within that space to eliminate the positive ions. This generally makes the space feel much better. (Labs, 1996)

Spirits – These can be ghosts or other non-physical entities which exist alongside us.

Universe – This term is used as one of many to Universal Consciousness, God, Source, Spirit (different than the spirits listed above), your higher intelligence, etc. There is no religious dogma necessarily associated with this term. It refers to whatever higher intelligence you may believe in, including your own higher self.

Vortex – The mass energy created by the people working in a circle. This energy accumulates and can be directed by the group rather than on an individual basis.

What are Vibrations?

Many people today are talking about "Raising Their Vibrations." They say "Meditate your way to happiness", "Relax and allowing life to flow", and "Raising your vibration for spiritual fulfillment." But what does it all really mean? Why should anyone care? Why would anyone want to spend their time on something so esoteric that it is hard to understand, let alone do? Why are these people so gung-ho about doing it, and wanting everyone on the planet to join in?

I believe that once you truly understand how energy works and why it is beneficial, you will start playing with it yourself and start to affect your own life.

Many people today are talking about energy work, they just may not realize it. Many magazines including TIME (MacMillan, Yoga and Meditation Can Change Your Genes, Study Says, 2017), books, and journals like Harvard Health (Harvard Health Publications, 2011) all chronicle the health effects of meditation, relaxation and mindfulness. At the core, those are the fundamental ideas behind energy work. People say they want their house to feel better when they walk in the door. They mean that they want the energy in their house to be at a higher frequency. They say they are feeling low or always tired. They are describing their own life force vibrating lower than is optimal for them to thrive. They want to feel better at work (MacMillan, Yoga Is Officially Sweeping the Workplace, 2017). They are asking for their work environment to not be so low vibrationally. They may not understand what "Energy work" actually means, but they talk about it and reference it regularly.

Energy healing is the ability to raise the vibrational frequency of the energy field that surrounds the human body so that physical, mental, and emotional healing can occur. Some people call this field the aura, some people call it an electro-magnetic field, while others call it the energy body. All these terms refer to the field of energy that surrounds the human body. This field has now been documented by science in several ways, including photographically, such as in the text *Capturing the Aura Integrating Science, Technology, and Metaphysics* by C.E. Lindgren (Lindgren, 2008).

Everything is made of energy. Atoms group together to create molecules. Molecules group together to create larger structures. Some form air, some form water, some form tables, some form the human body. If you look at the world as pieces of energy that are constantly interacting with other energy, things start to make sense. Since everything is made of energy, everything also has a specific vibratory frequency. Solids, liquids, and gases each vibrate at different rates, with faster-moving particles like air that are more unstable and slower-moving particles, like tables and people, that are more substantial (Waikato, 2014).

There is another level of vibrational frequency that occurs with living things. All living things, including plants, have a consciousness. This means that they are aware of, and reacting to others in their environment. There have been many experiments performed on plants to test whether they react to external thought, such as in Annie B. Bond's article, "*Psychic Reactions From House Plants?*" In her article she discusses Cleve Backster, a scientist working with police on polygraphing. He decided to attach the electrodes of a lie detector to the leaves of a dracaena plant to see if they were sensitive enough to pick up reactions from a non-human subject. These experiments came back conclusively showing that plants are indeed aware of those around them. Ross Heaven and Howard G Charing also wrote about this phenomenon in *Plant Spirit Shamanism* (Charing, 2006). The reactions that we have to others in our environment will cause our personal frequency to change. Bad feelings drop our frequency, good feelings raises our frequency. What we feel in turn affects our thoughts, and those thoughts affect the world around us. Like magnets, we attract to us those things that resonate with the frequency we are putting out. The frequency that we are putting out can be easily gauged by our feelings.

The idea of personal vibration was made popular in the Western world by Rhonda Byrne's book *The Secret* (Byrne, 2006), which discusses the Law of Attraction and how people can access anything they want simply be becoming a vibrational match to it. It states that your vibration is what is causing your world to occur the way it does.

- We all work with one infinite power; Universal Knowledge or GOD, depending on your personal beliefs.
- The Secret is the Law of Attraction (LOA).
- Whatever is going on in your mind is what you are attracting, and therefore reflected in your experiences.
- We are like magnets – like attracts like. You become AND attract what you think.

- Every thought has a frequency. Thoughts send out a magnetic energy which attracts to it those things that resonate with it.
- When people think about what they don't want they attract more of the same.
- There is no negation with the Law of Attraction. It does not understand NO. It simply recognizes that you are thinking about something.
- Thought = creation. If these thoughts are attached to powerful emotions (good or bad) that speeds the creation.

Byrne goes on to explain that if you are in a low vibration (feeling bad), you will attract more things that make you feel bad. If you are in a high vibration (feeling good), you will attract more things that make you feel good. So how do you change your vibration? Pay attention to your feelings. The better you feel, the higher your vibration. If you just concentrate on always feeling good, you will naturally stay at a higher level.

This was a good start. However, raising your vibration is not only hard to do, but also hard to get your head around. Many people don't know that *The Secret* was based on the teachings of Abraham. Abraham is the name given to Universal Consciousness (or Universe or GOD) as it is being channeled by a woman called Esther Hicks (Publications, 1997). The story behind the name Abraham is that as Esther was working with this consciousness, she asked for the name of the guide with which she was working. Because Esther posed the question in that way, she was given a name to which she could relate. Abraham is very specific about the fact that they are not just one being. They are all intelligence.

When speaking to those who can tap into this intelligence like a psychic or channel, people usually like to ask "What is the name of your guide?" This question is flawed because it assumes that there is only one "person" that the psychic can access, and all the information they get must come from that one "person."

After releasing her book Byrne created the movie. Since The Secret was based on the teachings of Abraham Esther Hicks was initially included as one of the characters in the movie; but Esther's parts were later removed from the movie when Rhonda and Esther parted ways over a business disagreement. By removing Esther, Rhonda also removed some vital information from the movie, since the book was based on the Law of Attraction through Esther's knowledge. Esther, however, was not removed before a first release cut of the movie made it to the public. This is how Abraham-Hicks initially gained popularity. I encourage you to look up Abraham-Hicks if you are not already familiar with this work. You can start with one of the many videos on YouTube.

The idea of working with the Law of Attraction is nice, but what happens when someone wants to put it in to practice? Are there rules that go into actually doing it? How do you learn these rules? Do energy blocks play a role? What about energy block clearing? What is that, and how does it work?

As you can see, there was a lot of information left off the table. My goal is to fill in a lot of those gaps, and provide practical ways to work with energy. I also hope to de-mystify the process, so that the information is accessible to everyone.

Raising Your Vibrations

The concept of raising your vibration has been around for a very long time. It was first documented in the Ancient Vedas of India around 1,500 BCE. Around that same time, in China different variations were also being developed, and in Japan the concept was recognized only slightly later. Meditation gained ground as a Buddhist spiritual practice between 500-600 BCE (Wynne), with the first meditation hall opening in Japan in 653 BCE. Heinrich Dumoulin's *Zen Buddhism a History, Japan* covers this very well. (Dumoulin, 2005),. By 20 BCE spiritual exercises in meditation had spread to the west (Levine).

Today, many people in the West believe that personal vibrations fall into some weird woo-woo, airy-fairy land also known as the New Age subculture, and only concern the delusional. In my opinion, that is not the case. Quantum physicists are now claiming that there is no universe without an observer. Austrian physicist Erwin Schrödinger discussed this years ago in his famous cat experiment, also known as "Schrödinger's cat." He claimed that until it was observed, the cat was simultaneously alive and dead. Since everything is energy what we think and expect to see definitively affects the outcome. The realities we observe consist of sub-atomic particles coming together and vibrating at different rates to create the universe that we see. (Bohr, 2015). Our human bodies are also surrounded by an energy field which is constantly influenced by our thoughts and feelings (Sharma, 2016)

Have you ever walked up behind someone and just known they were upset without seeing their face? Have you ever had a seemingly pleasant conversation with someone but knew deep down that you don't trust them? That is a result of your energy field interacting with their energy field. This happens in the same way that you can walk up behind someone who is sitting in a chair looking at a computer screen with their back to you, not moving or speaking, but you just know they are angry. You did not hear their voice, or see their face. They were not displaying any kind of body language that would tip you off to the fact that they are angry, but you just sensed it. You were receiving information from them through your energy field, and reacting to their vibration.

We receive a lot of information about the world around us, and project a lot of information about ourselves without any physical communication. The thoughts and emotions that we experience are what create our personal reality. I use the word create because all things being equal, two people who think and feel differently can walk into the same room, interact with the same people, and have completely different experiences. The people and environment around them will change to match the frequency they are putting out.

Someone happy, confident, and lively will attract similar people to them and will have an amazing time. They will experience a friendly, happy atmosphere and have a great time. They will most likely engage in happy, lively conversation and walk away feeling great. In most instances, they will not have interacted with anyone unpleasant or unhappy. That is because those people would naturally be kept out of their space due to the Law of Attraction.

Someone self-conscious, unhappy, and living in a victim mentality will have a completely different experience. That person will find that very few, if any, people want to talk to them. They will be isolated from the group. The other participants will not do this on purpose, they will simply be reacting to the negative vibration this person is putting off. As a result, this second person will walk away from the room feeling unloved, isolated, unhappy, etc. having had a less than ideal experience.

As suggested by the examples above, reality is very subjective. Both people had a very real experience. Both experiences are valid. One person would say the evening was amazing. The other person would say the evening was horrible. The world outside the two people was the same world. The difference was the people themselves. The vibration they were projecting caused the external world to change as it reacted to their vibration, and each attracted those circumstances that matched their expectations whether conscious or unconscious.

What is important to note, is that none of this happens at the conscious level. It is all caused by information that is sent out energetically by the observer (you), so you create your own reality.

This also works with luck. Have you ever noticed that some people just seem "lucky?" They have all kinds of fun and exciting things show up in their life without much effort. The Law of Attraction is working with these people. "Lucky" events and coincidences are high vibration in nature, and will therefore be attracted to those people who are matching that frequency.

Given this information, we can start looking at how vibrations cause realities. Scientists at MIT have recently installed an MEG (Magnetoencephalography) scanner and have started mapping out the specific frequency of thoughts (Levy, 2012). As you will see below, happy, relaxed thoughts measure higher on the frequency scale, while unhappy, stressful thoughts measure lower on the frequency scale.

Below is a chart from David Hawkins's book *Power vs. Force* (1995) where he measured the vibration levels of people, which he calls "Log", and the correlating emotional experience. Dr. David Hawkins studied energetic frequencies of thoughts and emotions, and using techniques derived from kinesiology presented a method by which one can gauge consciousness frequencies on a scale of 1 to 1000. On this scale 1 is simply being alive and breathing, someone brain dead may fall into this category, and 1000 is the ultimate state of enlightenment. As you can see he documented the full continuum of the human emotional range.

	Level	Scale (Log of)	Emotion	Process	Life View
P O W E R	Enlightenment	700-1,000	Ineffable	Pure Consciousness	Is
	Peace	600	Bliss	Illumination	Perfect
	Joy	540	Serenity	Transfiguration	Complete
	Love	500	Reverence	Revelation	Benign
	Reason	400	Understanding	Abstraction	Meaningful
	Acceptance	350	Forgiveness	Transcendence	Harmonious
	Willingness	310	Optimism	Intention	Hopeful
	Neutrality	250	Trust	Release	Satisfactory
	Courage	200	Affirmation	Empowerment	Feasible
F O R C E	Pride	175	Dignity (Scorn)	Inflation	Demanding
	Anger	150	Hate	Aggression	Antagonistic
	Desire	125	Craving	Enslavement	Disappointing
	Fear	100	Anxiety	Withdrawal	Frightening
	Grief	75	Regret	Despondency	Tragic
	Apathy	50	Despair	Abdication	Hopeless
	Guilt	30	Blame	Destruction	Condemnation (Evil)
	Shame	20	Humiliation	Elimination	Miserable

(Hawkins, 1995)

If this chart accurately represents how our emotions affect the frequency at which we vibrate, the argument for raising your vibration starts to make sense. When you are happy, you are more relaxed. You tend to have more expanded thoughts. You are more creative. You have better ideas. You are more able to act on those ideas and make the world a better place. You can relate to other people. You come from a place of sympathy and joy and can easily interact with others, thereby creating better relationships

Given all this, the desire to raise your vibration starts to make sense. We start to see why many power players have taken to meditating and other forms of mental relaxation. Walt Disney, Einstein, Thomas Edison and many others all meditated in their own way. They used meditation as a way to solve the seemingly unsolvable problems. Today Hollywood producers, Rock Musicians, Advertising Executives etc. hire experts to learn meditation because of its proven ability to inspire creativity and progress. Many magazines, including Fast Company, are noticing the value that top performers in all industries place on these practices (KAMENETZ, 2011). In order to tap into that knowledge, you cannot work at the lower vibration levels. Your mind will not connect to available solutions while at the "Force" part of Hawkins' scale.

Energy Work Throughout History

Energy work falls into two categories: Overt, and Occult. Unlike its common colloquial definitions, "occult" actually means "hidden."

> The occult, from the Latin word *occultus* "clandestine, hidden, secret", is "knowledge of the hidden". In common English usage, occult refers to "knowledge of the paranormal", as opposed to science or "knowledge of the measurable". Occultism is the study of occult practices, including (but not limited to) magic, alchemy, extra-sensory perception, astrology, spiritualism, religion, and divination. (Press, n.d.)

Many people also think of, and refer to, the occult as the "Dark Arts." If you look at the definition provided for "occult," all religions and their practices fall into this category. This includes Christianity, Judaism, Islam, etc.

Ancient Egypt

The word Alchemy comes from the Egyptian root of Al-Khemet. (University of Bristol, n.d.) "Al" meaning from, and "Khem" meaning black. Ancient Egypt was known as (and called itself) the black lands "Khemet" because of the highly fertile soils that were found there. Ancient Egyptians had very strong spiritual practices which were not shared with the general public. The rights and rituals were kept by the high priests and priestesses who lived in the temples and kept the traditions. Throughout the world the Egyptians' spiritual practices were known as Al-khemet or "Black Arts".

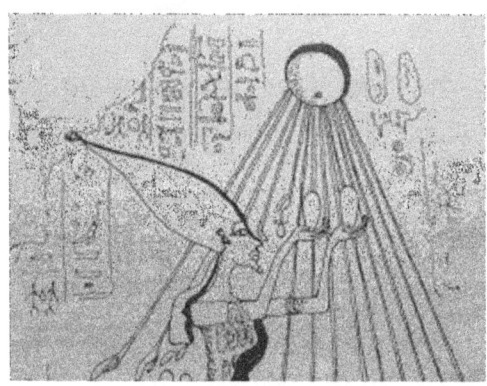

Fig# 1 (Unknown)

These spiritual practices included working on the physical, mental, and spiritual parts of the human. The Egyptians considered all aspects of the person equally important, and recognized that ignoring one would cause the others to fall out of balance as well. They worked with quantum physics, and saw the soul as the most important area on which to focus. They knew that once the soul was aligned with the body and emotions, the human being would gain immense power. The term Alchemy or "black arts" was never intended to mean anything evil or subversive. It simply referred to the secret spiritual teachings of the Egyptians. Interestingly, the term "Dark / Black arts" originated from the practitioners outside of Ancient Egypt.

Fig# 2 (Unknown)

The Egyptians focused on what are known as the 7 principles of Hermetics documented in the Kybalion:

I. THE PRINCIPLE OF MENTALISM.

"THE ALL is MIND; The Universe is Mental. "This Principle embodies the truth that "All is Mind."It explains that THE ALL (which is the Substantial Reality underlying all the outward manifestations and appearances which we know under the terms of "The Material Universe"; the "Phenomena of Life"; "Matter"; "Energy"; and, in short, all that is apparent to our material senses) is SPIRIT...

II. THE PRINCIPLE OF CORRESPONDENCE.

"As above, so below; as below so above. "This Principle embodies the truth that there is always a Correspondence between the laws and phenomena of the various planes of Being and Life.

III. THE PRINCIPLE OF VIBRATION.

"Nothing rests; everything moves; everything vibrates. "This Principle embodies the truth that "everything is in motion"; "everything vibrates"; "nothing is at rest"; facts which Modern Science endorses, and which each new scientific discovery tends to verify.

IV. THE PRINCIPLE OF POLARITY.

"Everything is Dual; everything has poles; everything has its pair of opposites; like and unlike are the same; opposites are identical in nature, but different in degree; extremes meet..."It explains that in everything there are two poles, or opposite aspects, and that "opposites" are really only the two

extremes of the same thing, with many varying degrees between them.

V. THE PRINCIPLE OF RHYTHM

"Everything flows, out and in; everything has its tides; all things rise and fall; the pendulum-swing manifests in everything; the measure of the swing to the right is the measure of the swing to the left; rhythm compensates. "This Principle embodies the truth that in everything there is manifested a measured motion, to and fro; a flow and inflow; a swing backward and forward; a pendulum-like movement; a tide-like ebb and flow; a high-tide and low-tide.

VI. THE PRINCIPLE OF CAUSE AND EFFECT.

"Every Cause has its Effect; every Effect has its Cause; everything happens according to Law; Chance is but a name for Law not recognized; there are many planes of causation, but nothing escapes the Law. "It explains that: "Everything Happens according to Law"; that nothing ever "merely happens"; that there is no such thing as Chance... only law unseen.

VII. THE PRINCIPLE OF GENDER.

"Gender is in everything; everything has its Masculine and Feminine Principles Gender; manifests on all planes. "This Principle embodies the truth that there is GENDER manifested in everything — the Masculine and Feminine Principles ever at work. This is true not only of the Physical Plane, but of the Mental and even the Spiritual Planes.

(Initiates, 1940)

According to the Kybalion this information utilized heavy symbolism. The idea was that if the symbols fell into the wrong hands, they could not be deciphered since the average person cannot easily wrap their head around spiritual ascension and removal of duality. It takes years of learning and practice to fully grasp the concepts of total connection, and involves removal of every day stimuli in order to allow the mind to reach for new realms of thought and connection.

For the Egyptians this also involved the use of psychotropic drugs. Their use of the lotus flower as a psychotropic drug was very prevalent, as depicted in almost every tomb.

(Fig# 3 Unknown)

Fig#4 (Unknown)

For thousands of years the lotus flower was used by the ancient Egyptians as part of religious ceremonies to reach higher levels of consciousness and connect to the Divine. In the ancient temples of Egypt, there is hardly a monument to be found that doesn't prominently display the Blue Lotus flower (ArchDrs. & Iles, 2005). It's seen everywhere on pillars, thrones, stone alters, papyrus scrolls, and on the ceremonial headdresses of pharaohs. When they opened Tutankhamun's tomb, even King Tut's mummy was covered in what has become known as the "Sacred Lily of the Nile," or the Lotus flower, seen below depicted with Isis *(Fig# 5)*. The lotus flower is actually a natural sedative. It contains small amounts of alkaloids highly similar to those used for sedation and anti-convulsant purposes. The Blue Lotus flowers were steeped in wine for several weeks and then used in sacred rituals.

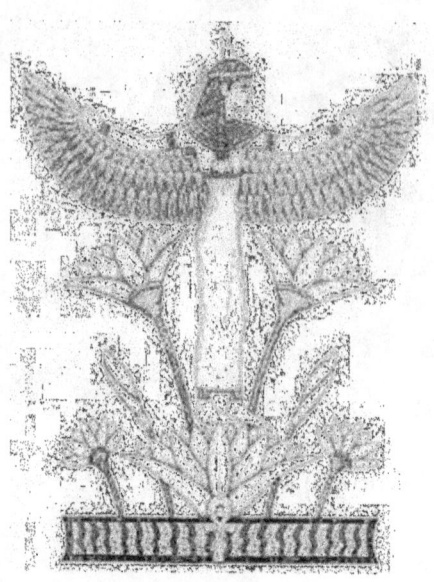

Fig# 5 (ArchDrs. & Iles, 2005)

As anthropologists gained a better cross-cultural perspective concerning shamans, the term shaman was broadened to encompass a number of different types of specialists (including medicine women and men, diviners, spiritualists, palm readers, and magicians) found throughout the world who are generally believed to have access to mystical beings whom they contact on behalf of their clients. Most, but not all, contact their mystical beings while in an altered state of consciousness brought on by smoking, taking drugs, rhythmic drumming, chanting, or monotonous dancing. In each case, the ritual involves a practice which shuts down the left logical side of the brain and opens the right creative side so the information can be accessed. While in the trance, the shaman becomes a medium or spokesperson for one or more mystical beings, a feature of shamanism in non-Western societies which finds parallels in the activities of professional channelers in the United States and western Europe who also speak on behalf of mystical beings for their paid clients. (Cabrillo, n.d.)

Roots of Western Alchemy

In Western Alchemy, the symbol for the initiate, or beginner student, is lead and the number is 1. The ultimate goal of the alchemical practitioner was attaining enlightenment which was symbolized by gold and the number 7. In order to achieve enlightenment, practitioners would have to pass through the 6 gates, or stages of growth to move from 1 to 7, or create Gold from Lead (Initiates, 1940).

When the transmutation symbol was made public, the general population thought the practitioners were trying to turn lead into gold. This misconception was exactly the effect that was wanted. It would discourage the average person from digging deeper into their secrets and rituals, thus the secrets remained hidden.

The Occult Path

As I was progressing in my energy work and starting to learn more advance techniques, I realized that there are very important lessons and rules that are not taught to beginners because at the beginner level they would simply not make sense. When I first decided to fully embrace the learning process and thought I was ready to jump to the end and just get it over with, one of my mentors looked at me and said two sentences that did not make any sense until I had reached the other side of the journey. She told me that my mind wasn't ready. She said that when my mind was ready, the body would follow. She also told me that all my questions were so linear that I would not find the answers thinking that way.

Those seemed like such surface statements, and it felt like she was simply refusing to give me what I wanted. She was refusing me the simple the education she could easily offer. What she was actually telling me was that I was still lead. I could not become gold just by deciding that I was gold. I had to pass through many challenges, and release many impurities in order to reach my goal. Looking back now everything she said makes perfect sense. I also understand that there is no other way to explain the process to someone just starting on the path. Like me, they will not be able to wrap their heads around it. When I tell other people the same thing, they have the same reaction that I did, and it is okay. I understand that it is part of the process they must go through, just like trying to explain calculus to a child. There is a lot they have to learn before they can grasp the concepts.

There are other important rules that beginners definitely need to know but that are not usually taught in their classes or by their mentors. This is because they are being taught by beginners who are just a bit more advanced than they are.

Many teachers out there have not gotten formal advanced training by masters in the field. They have not spent years leaning from those who hold the secrets. They have simply gone out, taken a 24 or 48 hour class, "mastered" what they were taught, and decided (or were told) they can then go out to teach others. My first few encounters with learning energy work were with these types of teachers. As I have gotten further into the study and practice of this work, I have also run across many people who claim to be well versed in their subject matter. When we start talking about what kind of training they had, how long they studied, and who their mentors were it usually turns out that they simply took a couple classes, 20 hours-worth of lessons at most, and then decided to go to work and teach.

All that alone would not mean anything one way or the other, but when I ask them questions about their experiences, and how they handle advanced situations that their students have, they are at a loss for answers. I rarely come across someone who has spent their life continuing their training in various modalities or research. Most people think that one or two classes is enough. They are not willing to invest the time and resources necessary to truly master the work.

I am in no way disparaging those who are educating the public on new methodologies here. I believe that it is very important to introduce people to new ways of doing things, and new ways to operate in life. The challenge is that most of them have never studied, or been exposed to, the advanced trainings. They are not aware of the fact that the advanced trainings are always, and only, taught by invitation. These secrets are not something you can pay $1000 for and spend a weekend learning. Think of the Shamans, also known as medicine people in indigenous tribes. They are trained from an early age in their craft.

> Shamanism is the world's oldest spiritual practice, utilizing a set of practical techniques that have helped human beings to survive in all continents of the world since Paleolithic times despite having no contact with one another. Although academics heatedly debate the issue, in our view shamanism cannot really be considered a religion because it has no dogma, no organization, no sacred book, and no recognized leader nor does it have a single founder. While people of many religions practice shamanism, Catholics, Buddhists,

> Hindus, Taoists, and Jews, not all shamans are members of an organized religion. (Practice, 2017)

The word *shaman* originates from the Tungus tribe in Siberia.

> Shamanism was first recognized by Western observers working among traditional herding societies in central and northern Asia, and it is from the language of one of these societies, the Tungus-speaking peoples of Siberia, that the term "shaman" is derived. In Siberian Tungustic the word is "saman", meaning "one who is excited, moved, raised," and refers to individuals who, while in a trance state, visit the realm of mystical beings to communicate with them and in the process gain mystical power. The principal functions of the Siberian shaman are guiding the dead to the afterworld, acting as a medium between the living and the dead, and finding out from the mystical beings what is ailing a patient or what the right medicine is. Shamanism among the Tungus does not involve the power to cure a particular illness, but rather only determines the cause of the malady. In this respect, the Tungusic shaman is a medical diagnostician rather than a healer.

Becoming a Practitioner

You cannot sign up for Shaman 101, or Oracle 99. That is not how it works. These masters did not take one months of their lives learning something and then know it all. They were taught slowly, over a long period of time. They were hand-picked by an "elder" who recognized that they had advanced capabilities and a desire to learn beyond those of the general public. They spent years learning and working before they were considered ready for the most advanced "occult" teaching (Cabrillo, n.d.). That is why it is called "occult." These advanced teachings are hidden from the general public because they would either not make sense to the average person, or could cause harm to someone untrained. Notice that I said *could* cause harm to someone untrained. When you strap on a pair of skis for the first time, and decide you are going to run a double black diamond course, *you* are the one who will be negatively affected, and your inability to reign in control may cause harm to others who find themselves in your path. Of course, there are always the random prodigies who will master something on their first try, but that is not the norm.

> *The shaman sees illness as a lack of power because it was lost somewhere in your life. In order to heal you the shaman returns your power to you. Other activities which shamans have traditionally*

performed include healing the land. For centuries, shamans have been involved with earth healing by using their ability to communicate with the consciousness of land, bodies of water and other such natural features of their landscape. Whether by determining why crops would not grow in a certain location, or the reasons for drought; working with growing things, the weather, and the land has been a traditional activity for the shaman. They would also communicate with nature to find plants to heal illness. Many South American shamans are responsible for discovering the healing property of certain plants, which later formed the basis for specific medicines we use in the western health system today. (Links, 2017)

The "occult" world is what an Olympic coach teaches. Imagine someone who decides they want to learn to ski. They go to the mountain, rent skis, finally figure out how those boots work, get out on the snow and move around in a zigzag line. Proud of themselves they sign up for a class, Skiing Level 1. They become good enough at the level 1 principles to stand upright and make it 50 feet without falling. Now they understand how to ski. They have watched people on the mountain and have watched every Olympics since they were born. They think they are a "Master." They have not, however, mastered all the rules necessary to ski in the Olympics, or to teach others.

I'm sure you can imagine where this scenario may lead. Not only could they potentially hurt themselves in the process by trying to show off, they may inadvertently hurt the people with whom they interact. They have not fully mastered the art of skiing. They have not learned what seasoned teachers have learned over many years of practice, failures, and problems that arose. They have taken a few classes, and may even know level 1-2 (how to stand up on skis, and how to stop) well enough to perform what they were taught. BUT, they don't know that what they were taught is not complete, and they don't know what they don't know.

The challenge is that many of the very important lessons are learned through experience. It is not until the beginner skier has fallen many times and twisted their ankles that those lessons begin to embed in their minds. Or until the Olympic coach tells them, "You are doing that wrong. If you do this instead, your skills will improve, and have you considered this other technique?", Or until they have experienced frustration enough times that a new idea pops into their head about a better way.

I had been working with energy for twelve years and formally studying for three when I was first invited to a shamanic spiritual retreat with a native tribe. I would be interacting with the tribe elders, and shamans. This retreat is where they teach their new initiates sacred rituals, and tribal dances. At one point we did a sacred earth dance to honor the Earth Mother. The natural phenomena that happened were incredible. I witnessed, and was part of, calling in a storm and creating rain clouds. This retreat was by invitation only, no one else was welcomed or given the location. This was my first introduction to the true secret world of the masters.

One year later I was offered the opportunity for an advanced class of only two people with another teacher. It was here in these classes that I started seeing the true power of the hidden teachings. I also understood why they are invitation only. Until you have mastered certain basics, you are simply not ready. You will not be able to wrap your head around the concepts, and you will not succeed at the work. You will spend the entire time asking questions that belong in first and second level classes, not there.

What I also started seeing in these advanced classes was that there are important lessons and rules to energy work which are not being taught to many beginner practitioners but should be. The reason they are not being taught is because, as stated earlier, most teachers out there are not aware of the rules themselves. These rules are fairly universal regardless of who your teacher is or what methodology you choose to practice.

This book is not a substitute for a good teacher, and should in no way be seen as such. There is really no substitute for a good mentor. If you don't have one, find one you respect and trust. This book is also not a prescription for any kind of specific work. This book simply covers the basic rules which would have helped me a lot when I was beginning my journey, and would have made my journey a lot smoother.

Accountability Matters

So, there are rules. And sure, they may make life easier. But why does it really matter? Why should you care about all these rules? I would love to tell you the answer is simple, but it isn't.

When you are working with energy, you are using a very powerful tool. You have the ability to affect your surroundings on many levels. You can affect physical, emotional, and psychological aspects of people. If you do it right you can help a lot of people in very "miraculous" ways. They will see it as miraculous, but that is only because they are not familiar with these powerful tools. Just like any other tool, the more powerful the tool, the bigger the responsibility. And the more chances of breaking something.

At the energetic level we all have free will. We get to decide what happens to us, when it happens, and how much of it happens. That does not mean that you cannot override someone else's choice. Just like with physical strength, someone who is more advanced is capable of overwhelming someone with less knowledge. It may not work well, and it will most likely end up backfiring, but it is possible. This goes back to like attracts like. If your intent is to hurt, you will more than likely be hurt.

When working with energy you must think of it like performing surgery. The person who comes to a doctor for surgical help trusts them. They trust them so much that they are willing to be sedated, rolled into a surgical room, cut open, believe that the doctor knows what they are doing, and most of all believe that they will wake up better. The patient is literally putting their life in the doctor's hands.

Likewise, when a client comes to an energy practitioner, the client is putting their trust in you the practitioner. By agreeing to let you work on them, they have consented to allow you to do whatever is necessary to make them better. They also trust that you actually know what you are doing, have their best interest at heart, and will not make a mess of it.

I remember working at a company that renovated hotels. This company got specifications from the designers and found vendors who would then produce the products that were needed. On one of the projects, the designer sent in a specification for a fire pit which would sit by a hotel pool. It had the drawings, materials required, location in the hotel, etc. We sent it to the vendor for pricing. The vendor responded with "You cannot put a propane tank inside that material. You are asking us to build a bomb and place it in the middle of a hotel. We are not in that line of business." As you can imagine, that little gem made it around the office, with everyone having a good laugh. On the more serious side, imagine that we had sent that to someone who was not fully trained in their craft. We would have surrounded a hotel pool with 35 bombs.

Using the above scenario, imagine the designer as the average practitioner. They have an idea of something they want to do and think it should be easy. They know that they want something to happen and believe that their way is right. Based on what they have been taught, the idea works perfectly. Now think of the vendor as the Master Practitioner. When looking at that idea through the eyes of a highly trained expert you see that the practitioner just requested a bomb. More importantly, they have no idea they just requested a bomb and are going to put it in the middle of a hotel.

I am not saying that all practitioners are building bombs and throwing them around. What I am saying, is that the watered down basic education being provided to the public makes people partially knowledgeable, but not necessarily educated enough to see the pitfalls, nuances, and variations, and how to avoid them.

I know someone who thought they wanted to learn a new skill. This particular skill would allow them to work with people at the subconscious level, and help resolve their deepest problems. This person took the courses on-line, without any in person training, and after the test was told by the teacher they were ready to practice on real people. I call those real people the guinea pigs. They know they are among the first clients, but don't know they are being used as guinea pigs. This practitioner did not, however, actually know what they were doing. I heard that almost everyone who went in for a session with them ended up being traumatized in some way. This practitioner was causing harm and not accepting accountability for the effects of their work. It took other more advanced practitioners and multiple sessions to clean up the damage that was done to the guinea pigs.

Kundalini Yoga

Kundalini Yoga has become a very popular and common practice these days. The idea behind this practice is to try to raise the Kundalini energy so you can reach enlightenment (becoming psychic is what most people think will happen to them). This is a huge mistake. What I have very rarely heard taught by the Kundalini teachers is the effects of raising the Kundalini on the body. When this happens, if the practitioner is not ready on all levels, it floods their physical body with all kinds of hormones and chemicals. It can shock and overwhelm your system. There have been cases where people have ended up in psychiatric wards for the rest of their lives from the physical hormonal disruption that happened to their system, and the psychological trauma this caused. Uninformed practitioners and teachers building bombs and setting them off.

I want you to understand how important it is to fully understand what you are working with when dealing with energy. Although the Western world considers it irrelevant, and ridiculous in many cases, that is just because most people don't truly understand the power of what they are dealing with.

When working on someone else's energy, you have been given permission to do things that can help and harm. Just because you don't intend to harm them does not mean you can't or won't. It is very important to be careful, and at minimum know the basic rules. Conversely, that person's energy is also interacting with you and yours. It is a two-way conversation. Make sure it is a good and healthy conversation rather than a series of misunderstandings or an escalating argument.

One day I was driving to a class and started wondering whether or not I was able to raise someone else's Kundalini. Once you have become advanced enough, you may gain the ability to pass this on to others. I heard "Yes, but you are not ready." So I moved on and forgot about that. A few months later I was having dinner with a friend talking about raising Kundalini and all the interesting things that happen once the energy is moved. My friend off-handedly said that it sounded like fun and she wanted to have that happen too. A few weeks later she started complaining of headaches and her body overheating. She did not understand what was happening. This kept going for a few months. She tried herbs to calm down her hormones. She tried meditation. Nothing would make the problem go away.

One day I got a text from our mentor who told me about a healing session she had with this friend of mine. It seems that during our dinner, when my friend had said she wanted her Kundalini raised, my energy said "Sure, why not, I can do that for you." On a subconscious level I had started the activation on her without realizing I was doing it. This was a huge problem because she was not ready, and I did not know it was happening.

There was no control in place to prevent the negative effects of the work. I have since then learned a lot about my skills, what to do, and how to control my energy.

This is a great example of what can happen when you only get partial training, but don't know you need more. In this case the energetic exchange caused a lot of physical discomfort to someone around me, and that problem went on for months before it was discovered accidentally.

Chakras & Kundalini

What the western world has been taught about the chakras, nadis, and Kundalini is incorrect. The origins of the names for the Chakras is from Tamil, not Sanskrit as many people are taught. Likewise, the colors that are taught today, are also wrong. The reason that people know the chakras by the rainbow colors is another example of trying to bring occult knowledge to the masses with little training. Since most people have a hard time accepting, remembering, then using information that they cannot easily wrap their heads around, the rainbow colors were used. It was an easy way for the kundalini and chakra information to be disseminated to the Western world, and accepted by the masses.

The chakra and kundalini system was first documented in Tamil. For political purposes and to control the knowledge, the Arya-Brahmins who translated it to Sanskrit, modified and copied Tamil literature then destroyed many of the original texts. This allowed them to maintain control of the information and how it was disseminated.

The Chakras

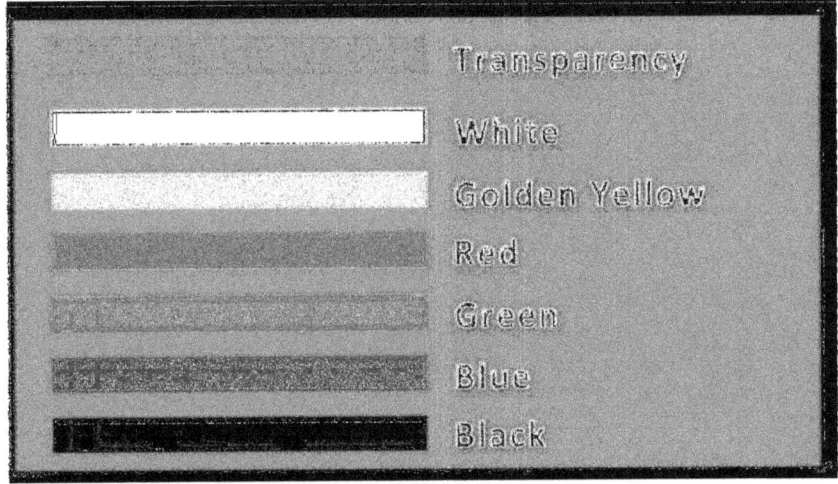

Chakra 1 – Black

Mooladhara Chakra is derived from (Moolam) meaning origin or base, and (Adharam) meaning support. This Chakra is associated with, and controls, the adrenal glands. It controls the organs that offer basic support to functions of the body. This includes controlling blood pressure, and regulating the metabolism. Origin is also where this Chakra's color is derived. Most things originate in darkness. The seeds of plants grow inside the ground, where it is dark. Babies gestate in the uterus, again, a dark space.

Chakra 2 – Blue

Suvathisthana Chakra is derived from (Sukkilam) meaning sperm, (Vathi) meaning residing, and (Thanam) meaning place. This Chakra is associated with sex. The origins of the term "Blue language" and "Blue films" also known as porn comes from this Chakra.

Chakra 3 – Green

Manipooraham Chakra is derived from (Mani) meaning time, (Poorthi) meaning complete, and (Aham) meaning body. This chakra is associated with the pancreas, and controls the exocrine and endocrine systems. These systems provide time keeping functions in the body. All symbols for "time to go" today are associated with green. When you are in traffic and it is time to go, the light turns green. This chakra's color may have also come from agriculture, where healthy and vital plants are green. When the plants are no longer healthy and alive, their color changes.

Chakra 4 – Red

Anaahatha Chakra is derived from (Anal) meaning Fire, and (Kaaththa) meaning Protecting. This chakra protects the fire which keeps the proper temperature of the body. Without this function we would fall into hypothermia and die. It also helps bring nutrients to the cells, and remove toxins from the body. This chakra represents both the heart and Thymus glands. The color comes from the color of the heart, and the blood being pumped by the heart. It also represents the color of hot coals, which keep a fire alive.

Chakra 5 – Golden Yellow

Visuddhi Chakra is derived from (Vee) meaning great, and (Suddha) meaning clean. This chakra controls the thyroid gland. It helps burn the body's fuel, once it has been delivered by the 4th chakra. It also removes fat from the cells of the body. If the thyroid gland is not functioning properly, you will not be able to keep a normal body mass. This chakra's color is derived from the color of gold. Gold is the purest element. It does not react with any other metal. This makes gold pure, and therefore representative of cleanliness.

Chakra 6 – White

Ajna Chakra is often pronounced as "Agnai." The name comes from (Aaku) meaning make, and (Neigh) meaning Ghee. It is believed that this name was derived from the fact that DMT looks like ghee. Ajna is associated with the Pineal Gland, the Thalamus, and the Pituitary Gland. Together they make up the 3rd eye. These 3 glands control the functions of all the other glands. They also performing the following duties: Regulating the endocrine functions, conversion of nervous system signals to endocrine signals, sensing day and night and controlling the bio-rhythm of the body, influencing sexual development, sensory and motor relay functions, and they are the controlling center for autonomic functions. The Pineal Gland also releases DMT, known as the spirit molecule, which allows people to see the un-seeable. DMT has similar physical characteristics to Ghee. In Tamil Ghee is called Neigh pronounced (nay). In Tamil the word Nouigh pronounced (no-ee) means fine particles. DMT also distills into such fine particles, and has the same coloring as ghee. Since enlightenment means "Lighting up your consciousness," the color of this chakra is appropriately white.

Chakra 7 – Transparent

Sahasrara Chakra is derived from (Sa) long, (Asura) gigantic, and (Aram) Spoke. Long gigantic spoked wheel, or wheel of great reach. The proper name for this chakra in Tamil is (Thuriam) which means fountain. It may mean fountain of DMT molecules, which links us with the astral world. Chakra 7 is situated above the head, communicating with the spirits. Since spirits have no physical shape, and cannot be seen with the physical eyes, it would make sense that this chakra has no visible color and is transparent. It is often depicted as a halo spinning above and behind the heads of saints, gods, and other religious figures. Since this chakra is spiritual, not physical, it does not govern any part of the body. It utilizes the DMT to communicate with the spiritual world, and translate those messages into a format that we can understand.

The Kundalini Pathway

Ida

Ida comes from (Idam) meaning left. In the body, the left side is considered the feminine. The Ida starts on the left side at the base of the spine and climbs in a snake like fashion through all the chakras to the 7th chakra where Shiva resides. There it meets the Pingala to cause enlightenment. The Ida is said to be linked to the Pituitary gland.

Pingala

There are two options as to the origins of this name. The first is (PinKalam) back vessel. Since the Pineal gland sits in the back of the brain, and emits the DMT, it may have been named for this. The second option is (Vin) astral world, and (Kalam) vessel, or (VinKalam). When changed to Saskrit, it could have ended up as Pingalam, then shortened to Pingala. The Pingala is associated with the right, masculine, side of the body. Pingala is said to be linked to the Pineal Gland. The Pingala starts at the right side at the base of the spine, and climbs in a snakelike fashion through all the chakras to the 7th chakra where Shiva resides. There it meets Ida and causes enlightenment.

Susuma

Susuma comes from (Su) great, and (Sama) neutral. This is considered neither masculine, nor feminine. The Susuma is the central nadi, or channel, along which the Ida and Pingala climb. You can think of the Susuma as the ladder they use to get to the top. This ladder has a rung at each chakra, so Ida and Pingala meet and cross at each chakra on their way up. When this happens, they fully activate that chakra, and clear it of all negative energy. Susuma nadi is linked to the hypothalamus.

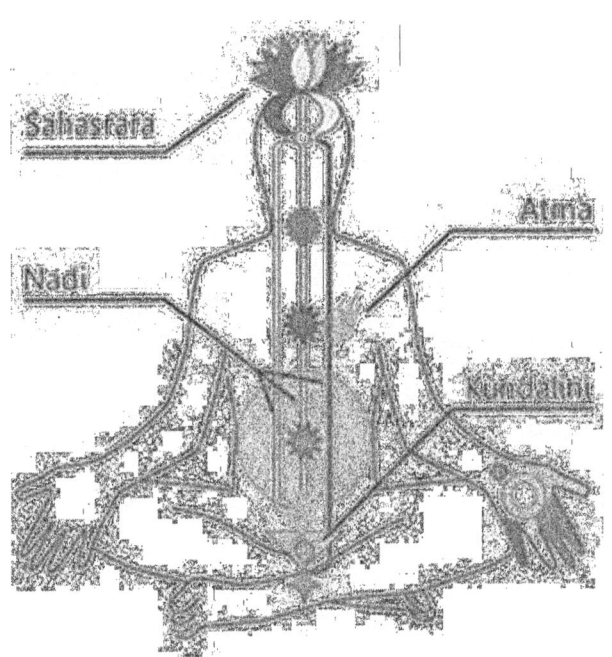

Kundalini

The Kundalini energy is described as a serpent which, when awakened, climbs from the base of the spine to the 7th chakra where it awakens consciousness.

Shakti

The Shakti energy known as Kundalini symbolizes the feminine principle, the activating power and energy. She lies coiled and dormant at the base of the spine waiting to be reunited with Lord Shiva at the 7th chakra, or Sahasrara. Shakti is the maternal principle – the provider, abundance. In the human as well as in the animal kingdom the mother offers nourishment, warmth and security. Once awakened, Shakti climbs through the Ida, Pingala, and Susuma nadis (or chakras) to reach Shiva. When they are united, enlightenment is attained.

Shiva

Shiva symbolizes consciousness, the masculine principle. He waits at the 7th chakra for Shakti to awaken, and meet him. Shiva is pure consciousness – the unchanging, unlimited and unswayable observer. Shiva has no desires whatsoever; these are inherent only in Shakti. Shiva is the empty, clear screen onto which Shakti projects her colorful film. Once they are united, enlightenment is attained.

Always Protect Yourself

My first encounter with formalized energy education was an Usui Reiki class. Usui Reiki is a form of hands-on energy healing which originated in Japan. It was the first to become popularized in the Western world, and has therefore become the most well-known. Most energy practitioners, who were not born with their abilities fully open and accessible, will start with Reiki simply because it is the most well-known, and move their way through different classes and modalities as they learn.

One of the first lessons in Reiki classes is how to connect with the other person's energy. Students learn various ways to connect to the Reiki energy and then to the client's energy before they as the practitioner start the healing session. What I learned was that you connect to Reiki, then connect to the client, then work inside a protected energy bubble. There were no further explanations given. In my head this translated into "Create a big bubble, and stick both of you inside it, then start working."

This same idea is also taught in another methodology that I work with called Energy in Motion. In that modality, the concept is called a "couple bubble." This does not refer to anything romantic. The "couple" is the practitioner, and the client. The idea in that modality is that you start by putting both people in a protected energy bubble, then start the work from a place of connection.

In theory this sounds like a good thing. You are both in a safe space, and the energy will work on both of you at the same time. The reality of doing this is quite different, and rather scary once you understand energy.

Think of your energy field as your personal immune system. It is there to keep you safe and protect you from random things that you encounter, and from other people. If you were to walk around not paying attention to your environment and repeatedly get cut, or put random things in your mouth, there is a good chance that your immune system would stop working, and that it would happen rather quickly. Once your immune system is compromised, you will most likely get sick. Now rather than just going about your life, you will have to wait for your body to heal, fully repair itself, then possibly prepare to start again. Depending on how sick you became, this may be a long process. It may also not be possible to heal depending on what happened.

If you do not protect your energy field, what you are doing is the equivalent of walking down the street taking blood and saliva from everyone you decide to work on, then injecting those directly into your veins. Everyone.

The lesson that finally solidified this rule for me was when I was working with a lady who had asked me to do some energy clearing on her. I started out doing as I was taught, connect to the energy and then entering the bubble together. What happened next was rough.

She had defenses in place to make sure that no one entered her field. These were not conscious, and she most likely did not know about them. I got through those with her permission. Inside those defenses was something really big and bad. This thing had made its way inside her energy and was using her defenses to make sure that it stayed right where it was like a virus. I saw there was something that needed clearing, but I could not identify exactly what it was. As I started doing the clearing work, the "virus" energy from inside her was being forced out. Once it was out, it came after me. Naturally I was not protected because I had put both of us inside the same bubble.

Thankfully, all this was happening during an open house that we were having in my office. We had split up the rooms in the suite so that different practitioners had places to do demo sessions with clients, so there were many other practitioners around. The energy that I felt coming off her was so overwhelming that I lost my ability to function. Now there was a client laying on the table, and I was physically unable to continue working on them. I felt sick and had lost my ability to think clearly.

Luckily, two of my mentors were at the open house, and available to help. I managed to flag one of them down. I brought her into the room and explained what happened. As soon as she took over, I fell to my knees and could do nothing more than fight to stay sitting. I think at one point I had to lie down.

After the session was over and the client left, I asked what had happened. I had never before experienced anything like that. She explained to me that because I had created a bubble around both of us, I had left myself completely defenseless. I had basically invited anything that my client had, to overwhelm me as well.

Here it is important that you understand what I mean when I say overwhelm. Energy itself is neutral. There is energy that vibrates at high frequencies and energy that vibrates at low frequencies. Beyond that, energy moves with intention, and it will maintain the original intention that set it in motion unless you anticipate and divert or deflect. If you have a negative intention, it will be experienced as "bad." If you have a positive intention, it will be experienced as "good."

When energy moves it needs somewhere to go, and it will gravitate to whatever is around it, usually a higher frequency sort of like a moth to a flame. Unless you are very clear about your personal frequency and maintain it consciously, it can overwhelm you. This also applies to guides and other energetic beings. High vibration beings or energies are experienced as "good". This category holds angels, spirit guides, your higher self, GOD, "The Universe", etc. Low vibration beings or energies are experienced as "bad". This category would hold things like poltergeists, demons, etc.

The name you assign to energy is irrelevant. What matters is the affect it has on you as a person. In order to not be negatively affected by random energies, it is important to protect yourself. An easy way to create this protection is to always see yourself inside your own bubble of safety. This is not complicated and does not need a lot of work or overthinking to accomplish. Simply intend to be in your own safe space whenever dealing with others.

Your environment also needs protection, and it MUST remain in place at all times. Create a barrier around your personal environments such as your home, car, work space, etc. Again, this does not take a lot of work, or require overthinking, and is not complicated. Simply intend that your spaces will always remain places of safety for you. Make it as big or small as you like.

The Lesson: You must always protect your energy. When working with other people, other energy, "haunted" spaces, or just going out into crowded spaces. You must keep yourself safe. You don't know what you are dealing with, or the original intent put into the energy itself. Always assume you will need a circle of safety.

Clean Your Energy

We all know the paranormal TV shows like "Ghost Adventures," "The Dead Files," and "Ghost Hunters." In these shows, someone goes looking to interact with "The dead," or something energy-based. They find a location that has reported paranormal activity, they show up, set up their equipment, and start trying to interact. They will walk around, talk to the space and try to get some kind of "contact."

These shows spawn legions of fans and "paranormal hunters": People who think it would be fun to hunt ghosts and play with Ouija boards in order to make contact with the dead. Why wouldn't they? The shows make it seem like so much fun. Buy a video camera or Ouija Board, start talking to dead people and see what happens. What could possibly go wrong?

What most of the TV shows never teach you or even mention is how dangerous it is to work with lower vibration energy. When you work with anything like diseases, injuries, upset ghosts, demons, and anything else which carries a lower vibration, it will work against you. All energy work is an exchange. No matter how well you protect yourself, you will always get something on you.

Think of it like using an umbrella in a torrential rainstorm where the wind is so hard that the rain comes from every direction. You will not be able to stay totally dry no matter how big your umbrella. The same holds for energy work. When you work with lower vibration energy, it will drop your own vibration. If you do not clean your personal energy field afterward, it will affect you. You must clean your energy after each and every interaction. If you have seven clients during the day, you must clean your energy after each one. You must also do a full cleaning at the end of the day. Not doing so may not affect you immediately, but it will accumulate.

Another thing to note here is that simply by raising your own vibration you will attract lower vibration energy. You may get "hitchhikers" that tag along after you leave a bar or happen to be out somewhere. These are lower vibration energies that see your high vibration as a big neon sign flashing over your head. They may need help, they may need energy. Either way, they need something and you have it, so they attach to you.

Disease

Disease never starts in the body. That may be where it manifests physically, but it always starts because of a "hole" in your energy field. When you work with lower vibrations, they attach to your energy body and stick to it. Depending on how low those vibrations are, they can start drawing on your own life force. At that point, you will start to feel out of sorts. Perhaps your mood will change, or become erratic for no good reason. You may start feeling tired or run down, again for no reason. What is happening is that your own vibration is dropping.

There are reports that some of the more well-known psychics become very unhealthy after a few years of doing their work. Some gain a lot of weight when they start doing mass energy work. Some started off as very nice people, but after a while their personality changed. Some are affected so badly they need blood transfusions because their body is so corrupted from vibrating so low.

The reason all these things happen is that they are not cleaning their energy field like they should. Either they were never taught that they need to do it, or they do not think it is important. Either way, their health starts to suffer, and they become less effective.

Lesson: If you are going to work with energy, make sure that you keep your vibration high. You must do a complete cleaning every day, and especially after working on particularly difficult cases. Your energy will not stay high if you constantly carry around dirt left by others.

The Rules are Only in Your Head

Every modality you will learn comes with rules. Some Reiki teachers tell you that you must physically touch people in order to heal them. Some tell you that you are never, under any circumstances, allowed to touch people in order to heal them.

Some people say that energy can do X or Y. We have all sorts of rules built around what energy can and cannot do.

The reality is that energy is not constrained by time and space. Energy moves with intention. Energy can do anything and everything as long as we have not set a limitation on it. Whenever we have a rule in our head about what energy can and cannot do, we limit what we ask of it. That is how we stop the energy from working.

One day I was working on a healing for a very large issue. We created a vortex of energy which we would then send to the situation. My role was to ground the group so that it would be safe for them to work. As I was grounding I saw several spirits in the form of elders enter the room in order to assist the work that was being done.

On that particular day I was in pain from a physical shoulder injury which seemed to elude any method of healing. No matter what I tried, this thing would not go away so I asked the elders if they would be willing to help work on my shoulder, since they were there anyway. They agreed and began working.

When the circle was complete and we were talking about what had happened, I told the group about my experience in asking the elders for help. Everyone in the room started laughing, and one lady said "Way to think about yourself at a time like that." She did not say it maliciously, it was done jokingly. What I realized was that in her reality, those that came to the room to help were only capable of doing that one thing. They could not multi-task.

In my reality, there was no reason why they would not be able to both help the circle and help me at the same time. To me, it was not a question of either-or; it was always both. I did not get any negative reactions to my request, and the work started immediately. Whenever you make an energetic request you will get an answer one way or another. If it is a no you will not receive your request. What I saw was that a request for help was sent and everyone who arrived was fully capable of doing everything that was needed. That included my need as well as the group's.

On another occasion, during a group session, the event leader told us to form a ball of pink energy in our right hand and put that ball into our hearts. I was in a place of meditation where my body was not responding, so my arm would not move. Instead of trying to force the situation I simply told the ball of energy to go to my heart, and watched it fly there on its own. After the exercise, while discussing what had happened, I explained what I had done. Again I received laughter. It had not occurred to anyone else to just ask the energy do what was needed. I don't think any of them actually accepted that is a possibility. Rather than working with intention, they were following the instructions of the group leader.

Energy can, and will, do anything you can ask of it. The only limitations to what is possible are in your head. The only way to get a solid understanding of this is to experiment.

Exercise: Whenever you are working with energy, try to find a different way of doing the same thing. Can you ask for it? Can you direct it with your body? Can you ask mentally, or do you need to say the words out loud? Does it matter if you believe it will happen, or can you just believe that it is a possibility? What happens if you ask but do not believe it will happen at all?

Start to play with intention and thought. Play with every aspect of the work. See what happens in each scenario and document it. Build your set of beliefs and faith based on your own experiences, not those of others. Remember, their experiences are going through their own filters of beliefs. Their beliefs are not "True," they are simply their beliefs.

Be Careful Who You Trust With YOURSELF

One of the first lessons you learn when you start working with energy is to be aware of what you are doing, and be educated about who you are working with. You must be conscious about what you are doing and your intention. You must be conscious about what you are creating. This rule applies to everything.

As you progress along your journey, your internal guidance will become clear. Some people hear their guides speaking to them, some see signs, and others just know in their gut what is right. Each person interprets energy differently, and this guidance serves you on many levels. One of the more important ways is in your interaction with other people.

Everyone has had the experience of walking up to someone new and feeling like something is not right. Maybe you did not trust them but had no clear reason for this reaction. Maybe you knew they were lying even though everything they said seemed to make sense. Perhaps they just made your skin crawl. There are also those people with whom you are perfectly fine. You like them immediately and you think it will be fun to spend time with them.

In each case you may not be able to put your finger on why you had that reaction to your time with them, but you just know. That is a very important piece of guidance that should never be ignored.

At the beginning of my journey, I sought out anyone who I considered to be a master at what I was trying to learn. Those who others told me were good and well-liked, and some I had never heard of. I remember one person in particular who mesmerized me as soon as we met. She was a psychic who seemed to be able to do everything that I wanted to do. I was so excited to talk to her and be able to work with her at a group gathering. I decided that I needed to learn from her.

She was confident and seemed to be in full control of all the skills that I wanted to master. She had her own business out of her house, and I thought that was amazing. She was able to work from home and do the work she seemed to have been called to do. I started scheduling appointments with her hoping to learn what she knew, and how she had the life I wanted. I was spending money I didn't have on sessions that were not very productive. It wasn't until a couple years later that I learned she could barely afford rent, and her finances were a mess. The life she seemed to have was all an illusion.

After our second appointment, I left feeling a bit run down. I assumed that it was the work that we had done. Anyone who has ever done energy work understands that it can leave you feeling drained. It can take a day or two to recover from powerful sessions, so I did not think much of it. After the third session I left crying. I knew we had done energy releases which can easily bring up tears, but this was different, I actually felt badly about myself. That feeling lasted a few days.

After that, I noticed that although my mesmerized brain was telling me that I should continue working with her, part of me was feeling a lot of resistance. She then offered to introduce me to her mentor, a lady who held classes which in theory would help speed up my journey. I tried connecting with this mentor, but the interactions did not go well.

From there, the relationship with that psychic deteriorated. Toward the end I had asked her a question to which she responded by berating me with a text message so long that it came over in 25 text messages. This was her attempt to control me and psychologically manipulate me into doing what she wanted.

This was a very valuable lesson about mentors. Just like guidance, the right mentors will never make you feel badly. It is definitely important to explore a whole gamut of possibilities to see what does and does not work for you. There are, however, times that you just know something is not right. If you think about doing something or working with someone, and a part of you resists, there is a good chance that is not the right direction for you to move in. In many cases you won't know if something works for you until you try it. I strongly encourage people to try on many different methods and teachers. That is the only way you will find what fits. I also strongly encourage people to pay close attention to your reactions to the things you are trying. The right fit will always feel good and easy.

Working with a mentor requires trust. You must trust that the mentor has your best interest at heart, and that they will not violate your trust. At the same time, you must give that person permission to work with you. At the energetic level, for beginners, this naively often translates to allowing them full access to your energy and mind. Once you have allowed someone access to your energy, you have essentially given them the keys to your house and told them to just come on in anytime they like. This is a very dangerous thing to do with the wrong person.

I have heard of people whose "mentors" call them up in the middle of the night telling them to wake up and do a session or buy a product, right then. The mentor claims that they know what their mentee is thinking and it must be dealt with right away. Of course these are always paid sessions, and the mentor demands the money immediately.

I have heard of mentors who claim the student's deceased family is insisting that they pay for this or that training. The trainings are held by the mentor, of course, and rarely by a party from which the mentor will not make money. I have heard of mentors turning students against loved ones who were actually trying to keep them safe. I have also heard of mentors energetically connecting to their students for the sole purpose of harming them. There are many con-artists out there, and they are only too happy to prey on people who are looking for help.

There are also many good and knowledgeable mentors out there who have nothing but the best intentions for their students. The trick is figuring out which is which. I personally have encountered both types. What I have found is that it is rather easy to tell if you have found the right mentor for you.

In my experience these are the characteristics of a good mentor:

> *1. They may show you things about yourself that could use improvement, but they will never demand that you change or make you feel badly for who you are. The information will always be offered as a growing opportunity, not as a way to berate you.*
>
> *2. Everything they offer will always be as a suggestion, and you will have the ultimate say.*
>
> *3. They will happily tell you "no." They will know what you are ready for, and what you are not ready for. They will not push things on you that you are not ready to handle. Like any good teacher, they know that the right time will come, and it does not have to be right now.*
>
> *4. They will sit back and allow you to come to them. They will never force you to work with them or spend money you don't have. They will let you set the pace.*

5. They will show you how to find the answers yourself. They may guide you when necessary, but their ultimate goal will be to empower you to do it yourself.

6. They will not expect to be your one and only source of anything. They understand that there are areas that are not their strengths, and will encourage you to find the right resources for those needs.

7. They will not be afraid to recommend other people for you to work with. They have a strong network of people that they trust and use for referrals. They are generous with information, including offering other teachers as resources.

8. They know who to trust, and more importantly they are trusted by others.

9. Working with them will never feel bad. They will definitely point out areas you can improve, but you will never enter a session with them through guilt or fear. You will never leave a session feeling worse about yourself or your life because of something they did.

You Can't Think Through It

I recently partnered with a couple friends to create a series of Facebook live shows where we discuss energy work. The idea was to create a forum that people can use to educate those outside the "Energy" community about what energy work actually is. Our moderator is someone who has absolutely no connection to energy work, other than two short sessions he had with me. His lack of knowledge is what makes him the perfect moderator for a show like this. He asks the questions that the average person would like to ask but may be uncomfortable doing so. During one of the shows he asked if I had seen the movie Dr. Strange. I had not. He told me that as he watched it, he thought of me and wondered if that is how energy work happens.

That weekend I went to the theater to see Dr. Strange because I needed to respond to the question about whether what is shown in the movie is comparable to what we experience. The short answer is no, but it looks great on camera and allows Hollywood to express their huge love of CGI.

In the movie, Dr. Strange goes to a learning center and asks to be taught. Once he is allowed into the school, he uses his intellect to read every book available. In doing so, he masters the energy work and makes "magic."

This is nowhere near how one actually accesses the subtler energies. You truly cannot think your way through it. You can read every book ever written. You can reach the end of the internet gathering information about energetic experiences, and you can talk to countless people about how they experienced them. What you cannot get with all that research is the connection necessary in order to access the subtler energies.

To reach the frequency necessary for connection at an energetic level, you must release. You must release all the emotional baggage that you have amassed and carried with you. You must be willing to release beliefs you have held for years. You must be willing to release daily habits and practices you have become unconscious of. You must be willing to release everything you know, and be open to the possibility that all you know, think, and do is actually wrong. I am not saying that everything you know is wrong. Some is, some is not. In either case you must be willing to release your resistance to the idea that you don't know everything. You must be willing to release your resistance to the idea that the way you have been living life doesn't work for this purpose. You must be willing to release everything. Only then will you be able to connect to what you need.

Many people set out on the journey of learning by gathering. They gather books. They gather information. They gather items like crystals, wands, and cards. They load themselves up with all the things their brain is telling them they will need in order to grow. The challenge with doing this is that learning happens through releasing and replacing, not through adding. In order to think in new ways, you must replace existing thoughts with new ones. Your brain will not believe that you can walk through a wall until you replace the idea that a wall is an impassable obstacle with the idea that you can make a door and use it. You can read everything about walls. You will find that they are big, solid, impenetrable . You will then come to the conclusion that there is no way to walk through one. But that idea is not "true." It is simply one way of looking at it.

Brain teasers are a great example of this concept of thought exchange. Take this famous brain teaser:

A father and his son are in a car accident. The father dies instantly, and the son is taken to the nearest hospital. The doctor comes in and exclaims "I can't operate on this boy."

"Why not?" the nurse asks.

"Because he's my son," the doctor responds.

In order to solve this brain teaser you must release a certain way of thinking and certain beliefs that are in your current reality, and accept a new way of thinking. Once you have found the new way of thinking, which allows you to solve this puzzle, you will never again be able to go back to the old ways of thinking which were released. The new thoughts have replaced the old ones; they were not added on top of the old ones.

The answer to the riddle, if you don't know it already, is that the doctor is his mother.

The connection to energy work and guidance happens in the same way. Many children around the world openly discuss invisible friends. They did not learn this in a class, nor was there a memo they all received. They simply interact with beings which many adults around them cannot see. These children are so open energetically that they are accessing beings which we would call angels, or guides. They not only see them, they interact with them on a very real level. At any given point they can tell you what the friend looks like, where they are, whether they are hungry or not, their personal preferences, basically anything and everything about this being which you cannot see. These interactions all happen in the right / creative side of the brain. You could say that it is all in their imagination, or you could accept that it is through our imagination that the subtler energies communicate.

The below excerpt was taken from a Psychology today article titled: Imaginary Friends – Are invisible friends a sign of social problems? As you can see, adults in the Western world see our connection to guidance and subtler energies as a defect, something to be studied in order to be "treated" out of children.

> Most young children play pretend games and interact with their stuffed animals, dolls, or other special toys as if they were alive. According to Marjorie Taylor and her colleagues at the University of Oregon, by age seven, about 37% of children take imaginative play a step farther and create an invisible friend.
>
> The variety of forms that invisible friends come in is a testament to the power of imagination. Tracy Gleason and her colleagues cite these examples from their research on invisible friends.

-- Star Friends and Heart Fan Club: "Groups of preschool-aged human friends with whom the child had birthdays, went to the fair, and spoke a language called Hobotchi."

-- Herd of cows: "Cows of many colors and varying sizes who were often fed or diapered like infants. Discovered when the child's father accidentally stepped on one."

-- Maybe: "A human of varying gender whom the child routinely summoned by shouting out the front door of the family's house."

As these descriptions show, invisible friends can be human, animal, or fantasy creatures. They may appear alone or in groups. Boys tend to invent only male imaginary friends, whereas girls have either male or female ones.

Children with invisible friends can readily describe what these friends look like and how they behave. Many children even offer details about hearing or touching their invisible friends. Invisible friends can sometimes be a part of the life of a child—and a family—for years.

(Kennedy-Moore, 2013)

Our Western society has decided that working with beings that are only seen by a few is not a good thing. From a very early age children are taught to shut down the right / creative side of their brain. They are told that their invisible friends are not real.

They are discouraged from believing in fairies, dragons and other mythical creatures. Some religions take this even further and forbid books and movies that portray the subject. Several years ago the Harry Potter series brought a lot of upset from certain religious communities. They claimed that it was evil and refused to let their children have anything to do with the books or the movies. From a very young age children are taught to disconnect from their creative, energetic side. Many times they are indoctrinated with the idea that these concepts are evil and should not be tolerated in any way.

As children, our lives literally depend on the adults around us, our caretakers, liking us and approving of how we act. If they do not like us or approve of how we act, they may not protect us and help us stay alive. Since humans are social creatures if left alone to fend for ourselves, without friends or the support of other people, there is a good chance we will not survive. From a survival standpoint, if the adults around you think that energy, imaginary friends, or just the imagination is ridiculous anything that allows children access to the energetic world must be shut down.

The connection to the world of energy and our higher selves lives in our imagination. It happens in the creative centers of our mind. All the work defies logic, and because of that it is blocked by rational, logical thought produced by the left part of our brain. If you try to access it through logical thought, your logic will talk you out of it every time.

In one of our Facebook live shows I was guided to speak about elephants and the circus. The inspiration came up the night before the show and was so clear and detailed that I had to write down notes. Had I listened to the logical part of my brain I would have thought that it was a ridiculous thing to discuss. It has nothing to do with our discussions and was actually a precursor to a subject that I had been trying to stay away from completely in our shows: organized religion. By this point I knew better than to argue with my guidance, so I went along with it, and on the show I talked about elephants and the circus. It turned out that it was the perfect subject to discuss that night. The day of our show, another one of the participants had been given the same message about elephants and the circus through a radio show she listens to. My message was not only a good reinforcement to what she had been learning, but led to a few more subjects which we would have not discussed without that catalyst.

Guidance comes when your mind is at rest. It does not come easily when you are power thinking. Many people who made great impact on history like Walt Disney, Thomas Edison, and Benjamin Franklin all said that they received inspiration while napping. They attributed their guidance to ceasing activity. The reason for this is that while they were napping their logical thinking brain, the part of them that judged, questioned and dissected every idea, turned off. In this state they were not only open to the greater inspirations, they had no resistance to them. The ideas were allowed to come and embed themselves into their conscious mind.

> *It is commonly known that sleep has multiple stages. However, Einstein, Dali and many others took advantage of just the very first one – the Hypnagogia, which means "abducting into sleep". Explaining the concept, Anthony Alvarado said, "Hypnagogia is that liminal in-between state where you are just beginning to dream but are still conscious."*
>
> *Einstein revealed that this half-dreaming, half-awake state helped his mind get flooded with images that were relevant to his research. Albert Einstein certainly isn't alone when it comes to napping. Anyone who has been exceptionally influential to the society has been a napper.* (Desai, 2015)

True guidance never shouts. It whispers gently. Many times, when first starting to work with the subtle energies, it is easy to mistake guidance for imagination. Mostly because that is how guidance shows up. Some people have brilliant inspirations and think they imagined the thought. They cannot see it as their connection to higher intelligence. They will start trying to dissect the thought and its logical validity. Their logical brain then takes over and kills the idea.

Personal Accountability

Regardless of where you are in your journey, you are in the perfect place. You are not doing it wrong. Yes, there are people way ahead of you. There are also people much further behind. The easiest way to cause yourself problems and slow your progress is to compare your path to that of anyone else.

What I have learned is that no one's life is the way you think it is. What you see is always their highlight reels, not all their problems. You don't see all their pain. You don't see all the mistakes they have made. You don't see all the hard work they did in order to get where they are. You see what they show the world.

I had a friend who taught me this very valuable lesson. She always seemed so happy and was liked by many people. She had that gracious Southern charm, right down to that ever-so-slight Southern drawl. She had a great job and never seemed to have a down day. She was always busy with this activity, or that concert.

What very few other people saw was her reality. She had grown up in a very abusive home. She had to go away to boarding school when she was young in order to get out of the house. Those things haunted her. She woke up in the morning and took pills to make her happy. She started off her day with coffee in order to keep her going because she did not sleep well. She drank coffee all day long. When she got home she switched to alcohol. Before bed it was another pill to help her sleep.

She would fall into spells of depression that lasted days. She once told me that she was so happy she had a job that let her work from home, because there were weeks where she would be so "out of it" that she would forget to shower. There were times when she couldn't remember how many days it had been since she had brushed her teeth. And all this was going on while heavily medicated in order to make her feel normal.

All that is to say, wherever you are starting is perfect, because no one is perfect, regardless of how their life seems to you. The road to raising your personal vibration starts with personal accountability. Until you can look at yourself and understand that you are the cause of every choice you make and action you take, you will not be able to master many of the beginner lessons, let alone the more advanced.

The Stages of Personal Growth

There are several general stages of the vibrational levels. The first is victimhood. Rev. Michael Beckwith, the spiritual teacher who founded the Agape Church, calls this Stage 1 – "TO US." The victim stage. Life is doing something to us (Beckwith, 2008). On Hawkins' vibrational scale this would fall roughly between 1 – 199.

People who are at this stage believe that they have absolutely no control over life. It is simply happening to them. Other people are constantly attacking them. They are always running late. They always happen to get stuck in traffic. Regardless of how hard they try, they can never get ahead. The car accident they were in was the fault of the other person. Basically, nothing is ever their fault or going their way. They are always the victim.

There is a very dangerous consequence to being a victim. If nothing is ever your fault, then you are always reacting and can never create. You will never get anything better than what you have, because you can't ever make a difference. Luckily, there is a solution, and if you are reading this book, you are probably ready for it, whether you are still at the victim stage or have progressed further. You are ready to take control of your experience and make it better, so let's talk about the practical steps to do so.

Personal accountability is everything. Without it, you cannot work with the energetic world because you have abdicated control of everything. It took me a long time to realize this, and it was not easy to accept even after I understood the concept.

My first conscious encounter with this concept was at work in 2005. It came as a result of trying to appease yet another jerk boss, and all the jerks I worked with. There was nothing wrong with me, you understand. It was all them. They hated me for being smarter than them. They hated me for being stronger than them. They were clearly jealous of me. Are you sensing a theme here? The truth was, this was a common occurrence in my life. I kept getting stuck with jealous, hateful, angry people. I never understood why it kept happening to me.

I once heard a talk show host say, "If you are walking down the street and run into five assholes, you are most definitely the sixth." Luckily I heard this years later, when I was able to understand what he meant.

One day, after displeasing my boss yet again, I came up with an ingenious solution. Something that would get her off my back for good. I walked into her office and asked if I could take an Interpersonal Communication class that I had found. I figured if I pretended the problem was with me, they would all leave me alone. I didn't need it, you understand, but maybe it would calm her down a bit and get her off my back.

Well, it turned out that the class was the best thing that could have ever happened to me. The first day of class, I walked into a room full of people who were really unhappy to be there. They had all experienced situations similar to mine, but the difference was that I had volunteered to be there, while they were all forced by their jerk bosses. I would have been upset like them, but I saw it as a way of getting a bad boss off my back, so it was worth the time. Not that I would learn anything, but it would buy me some peace. Regardless of our reasons for being there, we were there and had to make the best of it.

The teacher was a wonderful man who truly cared about people and their happiness and, more importantly, made a lot of sense. This class was the turning point for me. The biggest piece of wisdom that came from it was that I was the cause. It was all my fault. No one else was misbehaving. They were all simply reacting to me. It wasn't that they were all assholes and I was a victim. I was causing the world around me.

The way I was communicating caused everyone around me to react in a specific way. The key to this revelation moment was that I was READY. Until you are truly ready for a change, and sick of where you are, you will not do what is necessary to shift your world. You won't even be able to hear these messages. This is a prevalent theme in energy work. Until you are ready, you will not progress.

So I listened, and I learned. I started paying attention to the interactions I was having. Whenever something didn't go the way I expected, I looked at ME. I analyzed my actions. I did not blame those around me. I assumed it was my fault, and they were not misbehaving. Since that was the case, then they must have been reacting to something I had done.

Society's Role

We live in a society that not only tolerates, but encourages lack of personal accountability. Nothing is ever your fault. There is always someone else to blame. Not happy with how something turned out? Find the person responsible and make sure they are punished. We see this in the corporate world regularly. People using scapegoats to get ahead. Leaders rarely say, "I was wrong."

I personally grew up with a family member who, to this day, is incapable of admitting she is wrong. She will argue her point even when everyone else in the room is telling her she is completely wrong. I have only heard "I'm sorry" once in my life, and that was followed by a speech about why she was actually right. The reality is that she is like many people. She is not an aberration; her behavior is common. With role models like that, how many people are able to find the integrity to do something different? It is just too easy to make everyone else wrong. We are never told to look in the mirror and figure out how we contributed to the problem. We are rarely told to figure out what we did wrong and then own up to it.

So as adults, why would we? By that point we have become set in our ways. Our brains have wired neural pathways that are so set, it feels almost impossible to change the way we do things. This is where the expression "You can't teach an old dog new tricks" comes from. It is because most people find it too uncomfortable to change the way our brain is wired. It is hard, uncomfortable, and truly unpleasant. What makes it even harder is that being a victim is a blind spot for us. We can clearly see how the other person hurt us, but we rarely see how we contributed.

All humans are essentially ego-driven creatures. Starting from a young age we develop an identity — a self-concept and self-image — constructed of our beliefs and how we view ourselves. Most of us think of ourselves as pretty decent people, better than average in certain areas, maybe a little worse than average in a few, but always trying to do our best. We believe we see the world realistically, and act rationally.

When our own thoughts and behaviors, or the accusation of another, challenges our cherished self-concept, we experience what is called cognitive dissonance – a form of mental discomfort and tension. Cognitive dissonance arises when you attempt to hold two conflicting beliefs/attitudes/ideas/opinions at the same time. For example: "I know smoking is bad for me…but I smoke a pack a day anyway." Because our minds crave consonance and clarity over contradiction and conflict, we immediately seek to dissipate the mental tension created by cognitive dissonance. The smoker can reduce their dissonance either by throwing the cigarettes away and trying to quit, or by thinking to himself as he lights up, "People say that smoking is bad, but my grandfather smoked two packs a day for fifty years and never got cancer. It's fine."

When we make mistakes, the gap between our questionable behavior and our sterling self-concept creates cognitive dissonance. We can allay this dissonance either by admitting that we made a mistake and revaluating our self-concept in light of it, or by justifying the behavior as not in conflict with our self-concept after all. Here are some examples:

You think of yourself as an honest man, but you cheated on your last exam. You can either:

Admit that cheating is wrong and that maybe you're not as honest as you thought. Or,

Justify the cheating by saying that a lot of other students were doing it too, so it really just leveled the playing field.

Unsurprisingly, many people, when push comes to shove, lean towards option #2. When our behavior threatens our self-concept, our ego automatically goes into hyper-defense mode, circles the wagons, and begins issuing self-justifications designed to protect itself. The higher the moral, financial, and emotional stakes, the more our self-concept – our very identity — is threatened, the greater the dissonance that arises, the harder it is to admit a mistake, and the more we seek to justify ourselves to preserve our self-image. Self-justifications are not lies, where we know we're being dishonest, nor are they excuses; rather, we believe the justifications to be true, and truly think that they show we are not to blame. (McKay, 2013)

As you were reading that, did someone particular pop into your head. Was it you? You may have thought, "I know someone who does that. You just described _____ perfectly." That is a perfect example of your mind bypassing your faults, and looking at others' behavior. Now, take a few moments to look at you. Find the last time you experienced a problem with another person, but you didn't take responsibility. Can you think of a time when it was clearly you because someone else told you that you were in the wrong, but you dismissed them as "too sensitive," "irrational", maybe "a complete ass"?

Exercise: Who popped into your head when you read the above section? Was it you? Was it someone else? Was it both? Think through the whole scenario.

If YOU were not on the list of people you thought of in that scenario, you were ignoring your own actions and blaming others for the situation that occurred. You were playing the victim.

Now, think of a time when someone you know did something wrong and had the strength and integrity to say, "That was my fault. I am taking responsibility for what happened." Or maybe "I'm sorry, I was out of line, and I was wrong." What did you think of that person? Did it change how you viewed them?

Michael Beckwith summarizes the levels of energetic growth into 4 distinct stages. While these stages do follow a progression, they are not linear. This means that you can flow between them. Achieving stage 4 does not mean that you cannot go back to 3, 2, or 1. It just means that in one area, you have managed to rise to the highest levels of vibration. Although these stages are fluid, you must progress through them in order. You must master stage 1 before you can move to 2, and stage 2 before moving to 3 etc. The fluidity happens between the stages you have already mastered, and those before them. The 4 stages are as follows:

> Stage 1 - "TO US." The victim stage. Life is doing something to us. On Hawkins's scale this would fall roughly between 1 - 199
>
> Stage 2 – "TO IT, BY US." The manifester stage. We are doing something to "it." We are making something happen with our mind. On the scale above this would fall roughly between 200-350
>
> Stage 3 – "THROUGH US." The Channel. We are yielding. We are allowing. We are open. We are letting. On the scale above this would fall roughly between 351 - 599
>
> Stage 4 – "AS US." The Being stage. We have become aware that our life, and the life of god, and the life of joy, and the life of life itself is our very own life. On the scale above this would fall roughly 600 and above

(Beckwith, 2008)

I remember the first time I publicly took accountability for my actions. I think it was my original shift from stage 1 "victim," but I had not fully moved to stage 2. I also had no idea what stages 1 or 2 were, I just knew that it was my fault and an apology was owed. I was part of a team of volunteers that worked with rescue personnel. We would go out to crime and accident scenes to do immediate, on-scene, crisis intervention with survivors so that the government officials could focus on the work they needed to do at the scene.

After about a year on this team, I had been asked to be one of the managers, and was also asked to help teach the classes for new incoming volunteers. This was not the ideal situation for me, but at that time I was not fully aware of myself and my needs. I am an introvert. A fairly introverted introvert to be exact. For those of you who don't know what it means to be introverted, here is a brief explanation. We introverts can only handle so much "people time" because people time actually drains us of energy. We leave feeling depleted and lacking. After a while (the while depends on the level of introversion) we need to have quiet, alone time to recover. Whereas extroverts feel energized after spending time with other people and drained of energy the longer they remain alone, introverts are drained by social interaction and must retreat to alone time to recover.

Our trainings were held twice a week in the evenings. That meant that after a full day of working around people and having to create my own energy where it was absent, I needed to spend an hour in traffic and then not only work with but in fact teach another group of people. I am not the greatest person to be around when I am not in good shape, and apparently after a couple of weeks doing this it was clear that I had become a problem. I was so severely drained that I did not have space for anyone or anything. Without knowing it, my body language and tone were those of someone really upset. I believe "bitchy" was the word that was used. I know many people would be horrified to admit that about themselves, especially in such a public venue, but once you have accepted accountability for yourself and learned how to make things right, it is really not that big a deal.

I want to make it clear here that most people become "bitchy" when they are not in good shape. When they have not had enough sleep, enough down time, enough food, etc. I am not an anomaly in this regard. I am just able to speak about it openly without judgement or shame. When you see someone having a bad day, there is a good chance their tanks are below empty, and they are simply running on fumes. That is where I was. I was so far below empty that it would have taken me a week just to get back to neutral.

The head of the team took me aside and we had a very stern talk. He told me that I was not working out in that role and that something needed to be done. There had been many complaints about my behavior. What I did next was not really a surprise for me, but it seemed to send a shock wave through the whole room.

I stood up in front of the class, about 40 people, and apologized. I did not make any excuses. I did not place blame on anyone else. I did not give example after example of why I was right. I simply apologized. I pointed out everything I had done wrong, and made it clear that I knew it was all my fault.

I was afraid. My whole body was shaking. It was the hardest thing I had ever had to do. But I also knew deep down that it was the right and only thing to do. Those people had done nothing wrong. They had come in asking to be taught, and I had repeatedly treated them poorly. It was not my intention, but it was what happened. So I owned it. Regardless of the consequences they deserved an apology. After the class, many of them came up to me and said they could not believe how brave I had been. They would never have had the courage to stand in front of that many people who were unhappy with them and admit to being wrong. In their own words, they would have died.

This was the anchor moment for my shift. At that moment I realized how few people are actually willing to acknowledge being wrong. Even if they know they are, and they rarely do, they will never admit to it. They would rather die than say, "I'm sorry."

In order to be able to work with energy and raise your vibration, you need the ability to look at yourself. You need to be able to see what you are doing and how it is affecting the world around you. Energy is a very powerful tool, and if you are not conscious about what you are doing, you can negatively affect everyone with whom you come into contact.

In the book Zero Limits, Joe Vitale describes personal responsibility and accountability as it is used in the Hawaiian practice of Ho'oponopono.

> *"To be an effective problem solver, the therapist must be willing to be 100 percent responsible for having created the problem situation; that is, he must be willing to see that the source of the problem is erroneous thoughts within him, not within the client. Therapists never seem to notice that every time there is a problem, they are always present."* (Vitale, 2007)

When you are working with someone trying to help them heal, you must take full accountability for yourself and your actions. It is you who is doing the work. It is you who is setting the intention. It is you who are the "doctor," and the person with whom you are working is the "patient" giving you their trust. From here, you step into a place of power. If you are 100 percent responsible, that means that you ultimately control your experience. You are the one who calls the shots. If you are not experiencing something that you enjoy, you have complete power to change it.

This is where the process starts. This is where you start shifting from stage 1 to stage 2. This is where you can start raising your vibration in order to create a life you love. Once at stage 2, you can begin raising your vibration and looking for a path to the higher knowledge.

YOU Caused It

You are the cause of everything in your life. Literally everything. Once you get comfortable with that fact, you become very powerful. The reason that most people live a life that they don't want or like is because that is what they expect.

We live in a culture that indoctrinates us to look at the worst. The worst in people, the worst in ourselves, the worst in society. Everywhere we look we are taught to be negative. The news media has an interesting tag line, known only to insiders, which is very telling. Their motto: If it bleeds, it leads. This means that the worst story will always be what is presented first.

Those stories will also be repeated all day. The news media will also alter the same story to fit the particular market.

The below picture is in no way a political commentary. I am neither supporting nor opposing the stories or their subjects. The picture simply demonstrates the news media's agendas, and their manipulation of the public's view. Even though I chose WSJ for this example, this happens with all news outlets.

This image was passed around on the Internet by a particular news outlet accompanied by the claim that the *Wall Street Journal* had deliberately published one headline, "Trump Softens His Tone," in a pro-Trump market area in an attempt to sway readers away from the GOP nominee. The other headline, "Trump Talks Tough on Wall," was disseminated in a non-Trump market area to bolster support for Democratic presidential nominee Hillary Clinton.

While reading that, did you make an assumption about which news network I must be talking about? I may well be talking about its competitor. What are your gut reactions to each side of that thought? Does your preferred network encourage such a reaction?

One of my family members is a huge news and talk show junkie. She has one channel that she watches all day. She turns it on in the morning and just leaves it running. There were days when I heard a story in the morning, and all day whenever I walked into the room that same story was still being discussed. It was never a happy positive story or view point. It was always bashing of the situation from their perspective. She would be subjected to the same information over and over from different angles depending on who was presenting it.

If you are like my family member, consider this: You are spending entire days being indoctrinated into a negative way of thinking. This affects your life, your relationships, and the way you view the world. You may think, "I need to be informed." That could be true, but either way you don't need to be indoctrinated.

You don't need to be bombarded over and over again with negativity.

There is another important piece of information about our brains which is never taught but is vitally important to this discussion. Our brains are trauma collectors. We are wired to collect and store trauma. This comes from cave-man days when we needed to know all the possible ways to escape an angry tiger and get back to the cave safely. People moved from place to place, and the only way to learn new techniques was by hearing about dangers that other tribes had faced and how they survived. To keep us safe, we are wired to seek out negative information, examine it from every possible angle, and store it.

Our brains also keep this information readily accessible. Imagine learning about how to kill a tiger from another tribe, then not being able to recall that information when you needed it most. It is helpful and healthy to reinforce such information moderately, on occasion. It is debilitating when you get it twenty times a day.

Our brains cannot tell the difference between something we imagine and something that is really happening. That is why panic attacks occur in seemingly mild situations. Our brains start processing a perception as if it was an actual life threatening event. They force our bodies into fight or flight mode, and we are bombarded with all the same hormones that we would need if we had actually come across an angry tiger ready to kill us.

You may be thinking, "So? What is the problem? My brain wants the worst case scenario details so I can stay alive, that is how it works, it must be a good thing right?" No! It isn't a good thing, and here is why.

When you spend all day hearing about bad news, and dealing with problems at work and challenges at home, it gets into your subconscious. It does not take long to program that amazing and magical computer seated inside your head to only search for the bad. Once you start searching for the bad, you are no longer acting, you are reacting.

Are you reacting to everything as if it is a possible threat? In each moment rather than looking at a situation as neutral and dealing with it from that place, do you expect an attack? This causes you to treat the people around you as threats whether or not they truly are. Your relationships suffer, and so does your life.

Let's look at this from an energetic perspective. We attract to us that which matches our vibration. The universe always responds with a "yes" Regardless of whether your thoughts are conscious or unconscious. If you are constantly thinking, "I am in danger," The universe will respond with danger. It must, in order to keep you from thinking you are crazy. The universe does not care whether you think something is good or bad, it only cares that your energy is being spent on a thought. Since you are spending energy on that thought, you must really, really want it.

Energetically, if you are constantly worried about being late, you will attract to you those things that make you late. You will somehow end up on the one street with an accident. If you believe everyone hates you, you will experience people always hating you (even and especially if they claim not to, because that's just a show of pity or manipulation). Energy does not understand negative. There is no "No" in energy, or in dealing with your brain. Our brains, and the Universe, do not have a way to process negative. If we are thinking, "I don't want to be late," the universe and our brains hear, "I want to be late." Because they love us and always want to say yes, we will somehow end up with the result we were hoping to avoid.

For those of you who are more scientific in your thought process, this is explained by the brain's reticular activation system. This is the system in the brain that starts noticing the things you are focused on. If you are worried about your car breaking down, you will start to see cars that are broken down along the side of the road. If you are hungry, you will start noticing all the food places along your drive. This is because your brain will automatically pick up everything that is aligned with your thoughts.

Why is this important? Why should you care?

Each of our thoughts has a specific vibrational frequency. That means that with each thought you have, you either cause your reality to get better, or worse. You attract to you everything you are experiencing. You are the cause.

That may seem daunting. You may be worried about having to watch each thought you have and realizing there is not enough time in the day to do that. You are right. The easy way to monitor your thoughts is to check in and see how you are feeling in any given moment. More than your conscious thoughts, your feelings show you your vibrational frequency. If you are feeling bad, you are more than likely focusing on negative thoughts.

When you catch yourself feeling unhappy, the first thing to do is switch your emotions. Focus on something that makes you happy. Sometimes that is just not possible. If you find yourself in a situation where you are unhappy, and it is just not possible to change to a happier state, try changing to neutral. Focus on a mantra, your breathing, or pick a few words that neutralize your thoughts. Taking a nap is also a great option. I am a big fan of Ho'oponopono. The 4 sentences have a way of neutralizing my thoughts. If I just keep repeating, "I'm sorry. Please forgive me. Thank you. I love you." My mind cannot focus on anything else. The idea is to stop the negative train right in its tracks.

You may not be able to be happy, but you can definitely halt the downward spiral. Some days that is the best you can do, and that is enough.

If you find that you are doing nothing more than stopping the negative train, you are way ahead of most people out there. You have mastered the art of noticing your thoughts and feelings and controlling them, rather than being under their control. After enough time, you will find that rather than just stopping the train, you are able to redirect it to a better location. These are all baby steps. And each one you master brings you closer to maintaining a high vibration on a regular basis.

Energy Blocks

Everyone works with energy differently and stores it differently, which means your personal experience may vary and that is perfect. The one thing I know is that when blocks are created, they are innate to us. When they release, they are easy to see if you are aware enough to pay attention. I want to help you understand what is happening, and how to see / feel / recognize the shifts as they occur.

What is an energy block? It is an emotional event which, at the time that it occurred, was far too traumatic for you to deal with. This could have been a perceived trauma, or an actual trauma. It does not matter whether it happened or you just thought it did, your system handled it the same way. At that point, the energy that flows through you naturally, your Chi, stopped. It would have been like a high speed train going at 270 miles per hour suddenly hitting a solid wall. It was a huge mess and far too traumatic for you to clean up and deal with. Instead, your energy body and mind came in and saved the day. They are like the Biohazard clean up team that rush to the scene after a spill and clean up the mess in record time. They then erase all traces of the mess ever having happened by burying it deep in the ground, then erasing all evidence it ever happened including proof the train existed.

Imagine that the place deep in the ground where the evidence was buried is a huge bunker that has been dug up specifically for this train wreck, so now no record of the train wreck exists and life goes on as normal. Except that there are little clues. A page is missing from the train roster. A distant relative of one of the passengers is still left alive. No one really notices anything, but there are still some clues. Life has been altered just enough that it is not the same. A little while later there is another collision. This time a plane crash. Same agency comes out, does their job, and hides the remains. They hide them in the same bunker, on top of the train. Again, there are some small clues, and life is just a little different. This same pattern goes on for years, and the bunker has now become a mountain.

Actually several mountains, because there wasn't enough room in one hole to bury all the collisions. One layer upon the next.

When energetic blocks are created, they are stored in the energy body in the same way. They take up a space, have a mass, associated feelings, a shape, a temperature and physical sensations. The physical body is located inside the energy body, so they will be felt and experienced in the physical body in the same spot that they were stored in the energy body. Once one has been created, your mind and energy body will do everything they can to cover it up as well as possible, so you don't have to deal with the negativity associated with it. They think that it was clearly far too bad for you to deal with the first time, so this is for your protection. Some psychologists refer to these as repressed memories. The problem with that definition is that definition only covers your memory. It does not deal with what happens to your energy and body. We build layers upon layers of other protections to make sure that nothing ever makes us feel that bad again. These other layers are like the scab, and ultimately the scar, that covers a wound. The goal is to cover the trauma as much as possible so it never opens again.

When working with energy blocks, many people will tell you that it is like peeling an onion. You need to remove one layer at a time, and eventually get to the original problem. This is so that your conscious mind does not get overloaded at once and you are not re-traumatized. No need to create another five layers when trying to peel off one.

We are wired to be able to deal with many things both physically and psychologically. When we come across something that is so bad we can't deal with it, our defense systems kick in. They build something equivalent to a brick and deposit it in whatever part of our body was associated with that particular trauma. If your experience was that your heart broke, it will be stored in your energetic heart. The size may be much bigger than your actual heart, or smaller, but that is where it will be stored. It will always manifest in the part of your body where you felt the physical sensation. Same goes for something that makes us feel like we were "punched in the gut." That event will be stored near our gut.

Both our energetic and psychological selves associated with that particular event freeze at that moment in time. They keep the same age and the same abilities. They don't continue to grow and evolve along with us. Because of this, when we are trying to clear an event that happened when we were 6 years old, our defense systems will not recognize us now, how much we have grown and how much we can handle. Any time we come across something that threatens to unearth that 6-year-old block, our defense systems react as if we are 6 years old. We become that person who could not handle it and take on the mannerisms of that child. This is why people generally find it so hard to release blocks that have been created.

It also explains why a perfectly rational, normal adult may start acting like a defensive 6-year-old when something threatens to unearth that event.

Once created, a block will not just stay stagnant in your energy body. It will start affecting your physical body as well. It will cause physical and emotional stress, aches and pains, and even deadly diseases. Until you deal with the trauma "blocks" very few physical remedies will work permanently.

There are many people who can help you through the energy block release process, and are happy to. What is important is that you find the right support and get all the help you can. You may also notice along the way that the people who help you may change. Each person is only capable of helping you to the degree that they have mastered a step. Once you reach the end of their knowledge, you may need to find another person to support you through the challenges. This is fine. It is like learning math. Someone who has only mastered algebra will not be able to help you with calculus. That does not mean that they can't help you at all. It means that they will be great at getting you all the way through algebra.

After that, you will need to find your next teacher. Along with that, I would not start out looking for a calculus teacher if

I was still doing algebra. The calculus teacher may not be a good fit for you at that time. Depending on who they are and how patient they are, they may try to give you information for which you are not ready, and that may only frustrate you both.

If you are just starting out and find a calculus teacher with whom you work well, and who can guide you through the entire process, great! Work with them. If you find an algebra teacher and they are a great fit, great! Work with them. The idea is that you find someone who can meet you exactly where you are and help you grow. As your needs evolve, so will your need for different mentors, and that is ok.

I work with many people who say they want to get rid of their chronic physical diseases. The problem that they encounter is that in order to get to the root of the disease, they have to dig deep and find the original cause. They have to be willing to face the original trauma, feel the original pain, and process through it.

Our survival instinct will kick in and do everything possible to prevent us from feeling the pain. It was so bad the first time, it had to be shut down and hidden. Our mind will divert, distract, and manipulate us into looking in any direction except toward the problem itself. We will feel anger, we will blame others for our pain, we will start thinking irrationally, all so that we don't relive the pain itself.

Some people try to psychoanalyze themselves and consciously find the block. In 99% of the cases, the block is not what they thought it would be. It is not associated with the people that we generally blame for it. Everything we associate with that particular problem is just a diversion to keep us from dealing with the actual pain that caused it. What we will first see is the layers of protection built around the block. These are the diversions, distractions, and misdirection.

So, what do these blocks feel like? In order to release the blocks, you will have to experience some form of them. They may come up as physical sensations like an upset stomach or tingling in your arms. They may come as emotions like crying, raging, or hysterical laughter. They may come as actual physical releases like dry heaving or running to the bathroom multiple times. All of these are valid and good. I will go into releasing the blocks in the next section, but for now I want to describe some of the blocks that I have experienced so you have an idea of what you may deal with.

The first type of block you may experience is an emotional one. These will be experienced as pure emotion, be it fear, rage, grief, even hysterical laughter.

I once released a block that came up just like that. I had decided to work on a particular challenge I was facing and had the time to release whatever came up. I was driving to a theater to watch a movie, and the whole drive I was working on the release. I DO NOT recommend doing that until you have fully mastered the energetic release process. I actually don't recommend doing it at all, but definitely not before you actually know what you are doing. Seriously, don't even consider it. I arrived at the theater, bought my ticket, walked into a movie theater, found my seat and sat down. About two minutes after sitting down, still during the trailers, out of nowhere I started crying. This was the kind of crying that can't be stopped. It was an overwhelming sadness and anger that took me over. I was bawling in the theater, and amazingly grateful that the trailers were so loud I could hide the crying. This lasted about five minutes, then it was done. The release had happened, and the energy was gone.

I felt lighter, and exhausted. It was as if there was an empty space inside my chest cavity around my heart. It was a space I had never realized had been full, which was now completely empty. There was space rather than heaviness. I was also physically drained by the release. When these happen, they take a lot of physical energy to process and may leave you exhausted. I was so grateful that I had over an hour to sit there and recover before I had to do anything else.

The second type of block is physical. These will feel like solid masses around or inside your body. All of a sudden you will feel a mass that wasn't there before. It will take up space and have a very specific density. It will be unmistakable. It may feel like a lead bar sitting in your body somewhere, or a huge thorny ball.

One block I had manifested around my torso. When it came up for release it felt like my torso had been encased in concrete. It was solid, large, heavy, and constricting. It surrounded my torso completely and extended a good two feet away from my physical body. Releasing this involved actually moving this physical thing off of my body and sending it away.

The interesting thing about these blocks is that although they are always there, you will not feel them until you are ready for the release. At that point, the "invisibility shield" around them will disappear, and you will be aware of them.

Many times, people say that they want to eliminate a problem, but in reality that is the last thing they want. The problem they say they want to get rid of is providing something so powerful that they will do anything possible, on a subconscious level, to keep it around.

I worked with a woman who had cancer. She was beside herself trying to get rid of this disease, because she claimed she wanted to be healthy. We worked on her challenges, and eventually the cancer started going away. She was so happy to beat the disease, and was able to stop coming to see me. Not three months later, the cancer was back and it had progressed.

When we started to dig deeper, we found the real reason for her disease. Her husband was a workaholic. He was rarely home, and when he was he had no time for her. She was lonely, and sad, and wanted nothing more than her husband's attention and time. Enter Cancer. Once she was diagnosed with the disease, her husband started working less so he could take care of her. He started working from home. He was giving her all the attention she needed. She did not realize that she had created this disease so she could finally start getting what she wanted and needed.

When we released her block her disease went into remission, and her health came back. Her husband stopped working from home, and went back to working too much. Again, he was rarely home, and again she felt abandoned. She had lost the thing she most desired. She then re-manifested the Cancer because it was what was getting her the love she craved. She did not do this consciously, but she manifested a way to get what she needed.

Energy Block Release

Now you understand what energy blocks are, and you understand how they work. You think you have a handle on this whole game and are ready to get rid of all your blocks. You think you are ready.

I am constantly talking to people along this journey. I work with them to release layer upon layer of blocks. Many times I hear them say "Where is the map?" "How do I get the map that shows me where these blocks are, so that I can go in and zap them?"

They seem to think that I can just grab a picture of a human body and start labeling different body parts with blocks. That is the logical approach right? These blocks have to go somewhere, so what is in the stomach? What is in the shoulder? "My shoulder always hurts, there must be a block there. Which one is it?" The problem is that energy is never logical. It will never follow the pathway your brain says it should.

Think of energy like fat. Have you noticed that not everyone carries fat in the same places? Some people carry it in their rear. Some people carry it in their legs. Some people carry it in their stomach. Where the fat deposits is based on the individual. I can't buy a picture of a human, circle the stomach, and say "This is where you will gain fat."

The same applies for energy blocks. The place where they are stored will always be the place that was affected by the trauma. One person can be yelled at and to them it "broke their heart." For that person, the block will sit near their physical heart. Another person will have the same experience but feel like "They were kicked in the gut." For them, the block will sit near their stomach.

Working with energy is very personal and hard. The person who wants to release their blocks will need to be willing to do a lot of introspection. They will need to be willing to listen to their body and believe what their body is telling them. Many times what they hear will be completely irrational, illogical, and counter-intuitive, and that is most often how they will know they are striking on something real.

The next aspect of releasing blocks is one that many teachers and healers do not bother explaining. They either assume you already know, don't know themselves, or are unwilling to tell you because they may lose you as a client, and therefore your money. You MUST be ready and willing to release. On the surface, this all sounds reasonable. You have a block, you know it is in there, you want to get rid of it Let's Go!

Not so fast!

In order to release an energy block, you must open the thick steel door that was slammed shut and surrounded by a 40-foot-wide moat filled with piranha who haven't been fed in years. In other words, you must pass through the barriers that were created in order to protect you from whatever was so bad that your soul thought it would have broken you the first time. That thing that your subconscious swore you would never have to deal with because it thought you would not survive. All of this is about survival. If your brain sees something as a threat to your survival, it shuts it down hard and fast. Then makes sure you will never be at risk from the thing it believes will kill you.

In every single case opening that door releases big, bad uglies, and when they come out, you have to be mentally ready and willing to go through whatever ugliness comes out, and survive it. Herein lies the challenge. Your energy system (your soul) knows whether you are ready to do so or not, and when it is not sure it will test you. These blocks are covered in layers and layers of protection. When you say, "I am ready to release this thing!" it may peel away one of the top filmy layers. This gives you a little taste of what is buried underneath. Remember that this top layer is the mildest and easiest part of the problem to deal with. It is the Teflon-covered coating that you just slide past anytime you happen to move in its direction. It was placed there to buffer everything below it. It looks like a warm, soft kitten in comparison to what is below.

So you peel away a small layer, and see what happens. Generally what happens is bad stuff shows up. Bad feelings, bad physical sensations, etc. This is the stuff you need to work through in order to move past this block.

I know people who started working on their money blocks. Money is very popular for people to work on. They don't understand that money is just energy, so if you can't work with energy money won't come either. These money blocks are the things they had in place which prevent money from coming into their lives. They decided that they are ready to remove this block, and start working on it. Within three days their washing machine dies, their car breaks down, or they get a huge unexpected bill. Their first reaction is, "Why does this always happen to me? I am working on this block and it gets worse?" Then they go into a mental spiral which sends them into a depression and they give up.

What happened was that their soul said "Amazing!!! You are ready. Okay, lets show you what is causing this stuff to happen. You have a belief, and I can show you that belief. Here it comes…." If they were truly ready, they would have looked at the problems head on and analyzed what was happening. Instead, they told their energy that they are not truly ready to deal with the problem. So the thin filmy layer of the block recovers and goes back to where it was.

Every block is so hard to deal with, that in order to do so you made a decision to never deal with it, EVER. On top of that decision was layered a belief. That belief was not so healthy, so to cope with it, you covered it up with another belief. That one was hard to deal with as well, so you covered it up too. You didn't like those feelings so you created a conclusion about the feelings which was turned into a belief.

Your soul's test was this: I am going to show you the belief that is running your experience right now. It isn't going to be pretty, but if you can handle what comes up and see your belief, we will be able to move on to the next layer. Can you handle it?

I like to experiment with how fast I can release blocks. Once I started seeing how blocks work, I decided that I was not interested in going layer by layer by layer. Forget peeling the onion, I wanted to just get to the core of the problem. I'm a bit of an extremist that way. I also don't usually know what I am getting myself into until it is too late, so that makes life fun as well. So I found something that seemed like an issue I really wanted to release and went after it.

CAUTION: I DO NOT RECOMMEND DOING THIS, EVER!!! SERIOUSLY, EVER!!! IF YOU DO DECIDE YOU WANT TO TRY IT, I ESPECIALLY DO NOT RECOMMEND DOING IT ALONE, AND DEFINITELY NOT WHILE DRIVING OR OPERATING ANYTHING MORE DANGEROUS THAN A BED OR COUCH.

I am telling you this story, in part to scare you, so you understand how big releases can get, and how they can affect you. You need to understand that layer by layer is just as good. It may take longer, but it will feel better. In worst case scenarios layer by layer will be what keeps you out of the psychiatric ward.

What happened was one of the most intense nights I could have imagined. I knew it was coming, but had no idea what would happen. It was around 10:00 PM and I got into bed, thinking about the release I wanted to work on, but still ready for sleep should the release not occur. As I closed my eyes, I saw a scene play out from my childhood. This scene seemed somehow familiar, like some bad dream I had years ago but still remembered. This time it was clear. I was watching it as an observer rather than being a participant, with each and every detail crystal clear. I watched the entire interaction play out, something that I never thought would have happened to me at a very early age.

I knew the work had started. Once the scene had played itself out I consciously went in and became an active participant, but not as my younger self, I was my current age defending my younger self.

As I participated in the scene I was crying uncontrollably. My pillow was soaked, and there was no stopping the emotions that came out. I was overwhelmed and inconsolable. The emotions needed to be released and were coming out hard and fast. Once the scene had played out again with me at my current age as a participant, and I was complete with the visual portion of the release, I started feeling very sick.

Right there in my bed I started dry heaving. But it was energetic. Imagine going through the entire process of violently vomiting, to the point where you feel like your insides are coming out. That is what happened for the next 20 minutes right there in my bed. But nothing physical left my body. It was a complete energetic purge. I felt something coming up out of my stomach, travel up my esophagus, move through my mouth and be released. It was truly the entire physical experience, but the only thing that came out was the energy that had been stored inside my body, the block. You can imagine how I felt afterward, and how drained I was. The upside was that it happened on a Saturday so I was able to sleep a lot the next day.

This is the kind of thing that can happen when you truly release a block at the core without going through the layers. The scary thing is that it can be worse. I don't think my release was as big as they can get. If you are not ready for it, it can cause a complete mental breakdown. This is why the layers should be released one at a time. This is why your soul tests you. This is why it is hard to release blocks.

Your Experience Is Your Own

When I first decided to study energy work I was so excited that I started researching about it. I read everything I could about the Reiki classes I was going to take, and people who had experienced it. I wanted to know what happens during the classes, and what to expect. I googled Reiki experiences, and watched YouTube videos for days. By the time I got to class I knew just about as much as the teacher about the history of Reiki, and everything she would teach logically. At that time I was very left brained, logical, and linear in my thinking. In my mind, I needed to know everything there was so that I would excel at class. This does not work in the energy world.

We are so accustomed to showing up prepared, that we have forgotten what it is like to be open to experiences. As we sat through all the attunements, I was waiting. Waiting for the experiences that I had heard happened from other people. Waiting for my enlightenment to kick in. Waiting for the energy to flood through my body just like it did for the people on YouTube. The one thing I was not ready for was my own experience.

I can honestly say that a lot happened to and for me during that class. I can also honestly say that I missed most of it. I missed it because I was not open to my own experience. I was expecting my experience to be like all those other people's.

In the energy world, that is not how it happens. Each person's experience is their own. Each person has their own variation to what actually happens. This comes from the filters and views that we acquire. What I see is never the same as what my mentor sees, or what my students see, and it may never be.

When I was learning to mentally scan the human body for diseases, I practiced looking for germs, viruses, fat cells, diseases, etc. As I was learning this, my mentor told me that when she sees viruses she sees robots with jagged helmets. When I see viruses, I see a swimming shark, teeth exposed.

These are both accurate and fine. What matters is learning what your personal symbols are, and what they mean to you.

I have heard of teachers who tell their students that something has to happen one particular way. If the student does not see, feel, or experience the work in that exact way it is wrong. The students are specifically told that the only way is the teacher's way. That is completely untrue. This causes so many problems, because the students never learn to use their own intuition. They never learn to trust themselves. They take a class from other teachers and get confused, because the other teachers are doing things a different way than the first teacher.

Many times we get in trouble, and begin doubting ourselves, because we try to mimic what those who are teaching do, but their ways are not replicable. They see the images, feel the sensations, and hear the sounds that will make sense for them alone.

What you must do is get comfortable with your connection to your guidance. You must learn to trust your own guidance, and you must believe that the information you receive is the right information. Until you do that, you will not be able to proceed to the more advanced learnings.

Your experience is perfect exactly as it is, and there is nothing needed in order to make it any better. Whatever you feel is right. Whatever you sense is right. Information will come in from all senses. Your guidance will also use your imagination and dreams to pass along messages. If you are open to the message, it will arrive easily. If you are not, you will struggle to find the meaning or miss it all together.

In my advanced classes we had one class where we were working with DNA. The exercise was to find any genetic defect in DNA, follow it to source, and fix it. This was a bit of a lengthy process as it involved scanning the entire DNA line going back through time. Once we saw the problems, we were supposed to fix them and then complete the process. When we were done, one of the students explained that she saw many imperfections so she just handled many of them at once. She grouped them, removed them and moved on. She called it the cliffs notes version. She then asked timidly, "Was that OK?" She did not trust that the way she had done it was correct.

The truth is, there is no right or wrong. Your experience, the way that it happens for you is always the right one. The wrong way cannot happen. It is an impossibility in the world of energy.

Negative Emotions Are Part of the Game

I teach various energy classes regularly to people of all levels. One of the most common questions from beginner, and even intermediate students is "Are you happy and clam all the time? Do you meditate and just stay relaxed and loving life all day, every day?" They are always curious how I manage to maintain my composure during times they believe they would not be able to.

People seem to think that once you have reached a certain level of "Enlightenment" you fall into one of two categories: Either completely Zen about the world and everything that happens, or just relaxed and happy all the time no matter what comes at you.

The truth is that the way people reach higher levels of "Enlightenment" is by going through things that are very hard. They go through battles that the average person can't or won't attempt. They go through very, very low emotional times. They wage inner battles. They look at themselves first when something unpleasant comes up and work on themselves. That process is painful and hard. The reason they seem relaxed most of the time is because to get there they had to battle demons. They have a level of perspective that the average person does not, and will not achieve. They see life differently and do not get shaken up as easily as the average person.

The answer to, "Are you happy and clam all the time? Do you meditate and just stay relaxed and loving life all day every day?" is HELL NO!!

I am human. Part of being a human is experiencing the full range of emotions. We were not put here to be without contrast. How do you know what you want unless you know what you don't want? The way that you know what you don't want is that it upsets you. Any time you are upset, you come to a conclusion. You decide, "I don't like this. It does not make me happy." This decision, if you care enough to recognize it, causes you to act differently. It causes you to make different decisions. It causes you to grow. Every experience we have here causes our souls to expand, and that includes the negative ones. The trick is to not wallow in the negative for too long. It's ok to go to the dark side, just don't build a house there and start paying property taxes.

You are a human, having a human experience. Part of that human experience is going through really hard times. If you are very strong and willing to work on yourself, you will come through those hard times a better, stronger person. You may see the things you did that you are not proud of. You may face fears and other problems you have had. You may challenge yourself to dig deep and grow.

There is also nothing wrong with not doing this. It is perfectly fine to not dig deep or go through the growth challenges. They are hard, they are messy, and they hurt a lot. The growth challenges are what cause you to rupture and then start again from another level. Think of a seed growing into a plant. In order for the plant to emerge, the seed must literally be cracked open from the inside. It must be destroyed for the new life to emerge. The breaking is a destructive process, and destruction causes pain. It forces you to stop being the person you were before and become someone completely different.

Your vibrations are a moment-by-moment thing. They fluctuate regularly. There is no such thing as someone who is always happy and calm. Those people who do appear that way are medicated, or lying

True energy masters seem like they are always calm because:

1) they have made peace with the dark side of their emotions,

2) they know those emotions are momentary and will pass,

3) They isolate themselves during the hard times in order to work   through the pain.

This means you don't see them struggle. It does not mean they do not struggle. They do not try to fight the negativity that comes up, they surrender to it and find the lessons that come up.

> *"Precisely because the ego, the soul and the Self can all be present simultaneously, we can better understand the real meaning of 'egolessness,' a notion that has caused an inordinate amount of*

confusion. But egolessness does not mean the absence of a functional self (that's a psychotic, not a sage); it means that one is no longer exclusively identified with the self.

One of the many reasons we have trouble with the notion of 'egoless' is that people want their 'egoless sages' to fulfill their fantasies of 'saintly' or 'spiritual,' which usually means dead from the neck down, without fleshy wants or desires, gently smiling all the time. All of the things that people typically have trouble with – money, food, sex, relationships, desire – they want their saints to be without. 'Egoless sages' are 'above all that,' is what people want. Talking heads is what they want. Religion, they believe, will simply get rid of all baser instincts, drives and relationships, and hence they look to religion, not for advice on how to live life with enthusiasm, but on how to avoid it, repress it, deny it, escape it.

In other words, the typical person wants the spiritual sage to be 'less than a person,' somehow devoid of all the messy, juicy, complex, pulsating, desiring, urging forces that drive most human beings. We expect our sages to be an absence of all that drives us! All the things that frighten us, confuse us, torment us, confound us: we want our sages to be untouched by them altogether. And that absence, that vacancy, that 'less than personal,' is what we often mean by 'egoless.'

> *But 'egoless' does not mean 'less than personal'; it means 'more than personal.' Not personal minus, but personal plus – all the normal personal qualities, plus some transpersonal ones. Think of the great yogis, saints and sages – from Moses to Christ to Padmasambhava. They were not feeble-mannered milquetoasts, but fierce movers and shakers – from bullwhips in the Temple to subduing entire countries. They rattled the world on its own terms, not in some pie-in-the-sky piety; many of them instigated massive social revolutions that have continued for thousands of years. And they did so, not because they avoided the physical, emotional and mental dimensions of humanness, and the ego that is their vehicle, but because they engaged them with a drive and intensity that shook" the world to its very foundations. No doubt, they were also plugged into the soul (deeper psychic) and spirit (formless Self) – the ultimate source of their power – but they expressed that power and gave it concrete results, precisely because they dramatically engaged the lower dimensions through which that power could speak in terms that could be heard by all." (Wilber, 2007)*

When working with energy, many things are counter intuitive / counter logical. Logically, when something hurts, you want to run away from it as fast as you can. Your primal instinct tells you that bad things are to be avoided, so you do everything you can to not feel bad. This has you fighting and resisting those experiences. The problem here is that it actually prolongs the pain, not makes it better. In order to make the pain go away faster, you must be willing to fully surrender to the feelings. You must be willing to let them overtake you and overwhelm you. Energy needs to flow, and when allowed it flows fast. That definitely becomes overwhelming, especially when dealing with years and years of repression.

You can think of energetic emotional movement like a flash flood. If you do not get in the way, the water will come hard and fast, then move on. Yes, it will leave destruction in its wake, but it will be gone, and the destruction is never something from which recovery is impossible. When you fight your emotions, you are essentially creating a dam, but one that is not capable of fully holding back the water. You slow the water and it builds up behind the wall. It releases slowly, and takes much longer to move through. Eventually, if enough water has been built up behind the wall, the dam cracks the water seeps through faster. The dam is not reparable because the water just keeps coming.

All Modalities Work

There are many avenues to connecting with Universal Consciousness. They are known under the umbrella of Energy Work. Psychics, Channels, Healers etc. All fall under this umbrella. Everyone has a different way to access it, and understand the information they are getting. But they are all tapping into the same knowledge base. Once you know how to quiet your mind enough to allow the information to flow, it will come easily. Some people, see the information. Some people hear the information. Some people just know the information. The way it arrives does not matter.

In order to teach new students how to tap into this information, a teaching method needed to be created. Many people decided that they wanted to pass along their knowledge, and so came up with their own method of teaching. Each one of these methodologies became a class, and students started to learn.

Just as a reference point for how many different modalities there are, here are just a few for your reference.

#1 – Quantum Touch ®

Founded by Richard Gordon, Quantum Touch is based on the principle of resonance and entrainment. The energy level is amplified through proper breathing and visualization of energy flow in the body. The distinctiveness of Quantum Touch is that there is no energy transfer from an external divine source; the healing is essentially based on resonance and entrainment of energy vibration through breathing.

#2 – EFT

EFT, or Emotional Freedom Techniques®, is one of the easiest methods to learn. It is all about fingers-tapping on the acupuncture meridians in the body combined with positive affirmations.

#3 – Reiki

Founded by Mikao Usui, the word Reiki is made of two Japanese words – Rei which means "God's Wisdom or the Higher Power" and Ki which is "life force energy". Thus, Reiki means "spiritually guided life force energy." The method of Reiki involves channeling the universal life energy to stimulate the integration of mind/body/spirit to enhance the natural healing mechanism.

The uniqueness of Reiki is that a special initiation from the Spirit to receive healing energy is necessary for all Reiki practitioners. This attunement of to the Reiki energy is a form of ritual to reconnect with the Spirit before beginning the journey of healing.

#4 – Restorative Touch™

Restorative Touch™ is a type of energy healing that works on a resonance of the recipient's own highest potential, calibrating and aligning their body and field to that highest potential. Practitioners work mostly with their hands in the client's energy field.

#5 – Brennan Healing Science®

Dr. Barbara Brennan is a healer, teacher and former NASA physicist, and the best-selling author of Hands of Light. Practitioners work with the "energy consciousness system," which includes the physical body, the chakras, the various levels of the aura, the dimension of hara/intention, and the core star/spark of the divine.

#6 – Healing Touch

Healing Touch, also known as Therapeutic Touch, is a biofield (magnetic field around the body) therapy that is an energy-based approach to health and healing. Its uses the gift of touch to influence the human energy system, specifically the energy field that surrounds the body, and the energy centers that control the flow from the energy field to the physical body.

#7 – Pranic Healing

Developed by Master Choa Kok Sui, a Filipino of Chinese descent, Pranic Healing leverages upon prana or life energy to cure physical ailments. The practitioner works on the energy body or aura of the person. Diseases, which appear as energetic disruptions in the aura, manifest as ailments in the body. This is cleansed and energized thereby accelerating the healing process of the physical body.

#8 – ThetaHealing®

Created by Vianna Stibal in 1995, ThetaHealing is a technique that taps upon the Theta brainwaves as well as relies upon the unconditional love of Creator Of All That Is who does the actual healing work. It is a technique that focuses on thought and prayer. While the techniques of ThetaHealing are inspired from Christianity, it is not a religion and it is open to people of all religions.

#9 – Longevitology

Founded in Taiwan in 1993 by Dr. Tom Lin, Longevitology is a method of energy healing that opens the student's chakras to receive this universal energy. Learning any types of energy healing modality can sometimes involve hefty investment cost. The best thing about Longevitology is that learning this healing modality is absolutely free. Moreover, Longevitology practitioners are all volunteers and they do not receive any monetary compensation from performing energy healing.

#10 – The Wonder Method

Founded by Jody and Alain Herriotte, the Wonder Method is a gentle form of energy healing to awaken the core self, overcome life's challenges, and bring about happiness and peace in life. Alain Herriotte used to be working with

Richard Gordon in the practice of the Quantum Touch. He is the author of Supercharging Quantum Touch: Advanced Techniques and Quantum Touch Core Transformation: A New Way to Heal and Alter Reality. (Happiness, 2017)

Each one of the above has many, many variations. Reiki alone has over 1200 versions. The most well-known are:

Usui Reiki:

Mikao Usui was the founder of reiki, which is practiced all over the world. Hawayo Takata, a Japanese woman, spread the teachings of Reiki, to the Western world by way of Hawaii.

Tibetan Reiki:

This form of reiki is a powerful Tibetan method of attunement and combines certain techniques from the original Usui reiki.

Karuna Reiki:

Karuna means a profound feeling to alleviate suffering, with abiding compassion towards all beings. Karuna Reiki employs sounds, endowed with the power to heal.

These sounds are sacred and powerful. They can be transmitted silently through intention or chanting, to bring about deeper levels of healing. The power of Karuna Reiki is used to heal addictions.

Gendai Reiki:

Gendai means modern. Mr. Hiroshi Doi is the founder of this reiki. He brings a strong Buddhist perspective to the original Reiki teachings and how to integrate them.

Rainbow Reiki:

Walter Lubeck, a reiki master began this form of reiki. In this system, working with the seven main chakras in the body brings about healing. These chakras organize a body of light. This spiritual energy is used to heal and understand our true nature.

Five Element Seichem:

Alex Baisley in Canada founded this system. This helps us to consciously use the five elements of the universal life force or prana to promote healing.

Shamballa Reiki:

This system helps to cleanse, repair and balance the physical, emotional, mental and spiritual levels of a *person. It uses reiki energy along with many vibratory symbols and healing rays to integrate the energy..*

Kundalini Reiki:

In this system, reiki energy is channeled through the lower base chakra rather than crown chakra. This kindles spirituality and even helps the practitioner get over shyness, or recover from trauma and other negative emotions.

Imara Reiki:

The reiki energy is used to work on past life, repressed issues and helps in long distance healing. The practitioner is connected to ascended masters and angels. (reiki7, 2016)

There are people who spend their lives gathering as many certificates as they can. They believe that if they have a lot of certificates, they will be more impressive, and more people will want to work with, and learn from them. They go through all the levels, and get a teaching certificate, and then list that among their accomplishments.

In the 1980's people had entire binders full of different certificates. Hundreds of Reiki classes. Reiki for kids, Reiki for dogs, Reiki for poodles, Reiki for large cats, Reiki for small cats,

Reiki for kids under 5 years old, etc. Each one of those classes was taught by someone who learned Reiki to Master level, then proceeded to create a very specific class.

As you can imagine, with this many variations, it is impossible to learn every method. But there is good news. You don't have to. Every single one of the methodologies leads you to the same place. Your job is to find one that resonates for you. One with which you feel comfortable. Learn that one. One modality is all you need. One modality that allows you to tap in to the greater knowledge that you seek.

References

ArchDrs., P. H., & Iles, L. (2005, Januray). *The Lotus in Ancient Egypt.* Retrieved from Isis, Lotus of Alexandria Lyceum: https://sites.google.com/site/isislotusofalexandrialyceum/the-lotus-in-ancient-egypt

Beckwith, M. B. (2008). life visioning [Recorded by M. B. Beckwith].

Bohr, N. (2015, June 3). *New Mind Blowing Experiment Confirms that Reality Doesn't Exist If You Are Not Looking At It.* Retrieved from The Mind Unleashed Uncover Your True Potential: http://themindunleashed.com/2015/06/new-mind-blowing-experiment-confirms-that-reality-doesnt-exist-if-you-are-not-looking-at-it.html

Bond, a. B. (2005, November 10). *Psychic Reactions From House Plants?* Retrieved from Care2: http://www.care2.com/greenliving/psychic-reactions-from-house-plants.html

Byrne, R. (2006). *The Secret.* New York, NY, USA: Atria Books, Beyond Words Publishing Inc.

Cabrillo. (n.d.). *The Shaman: A poorly understood, fascinating, and useful ancient universal role.* Retrieved from Cabrillo.edu: https://www.cabrillo.edu/~crsmith/shaman.html

Charing, H. G. (2006). *Plant Spirit Shamanism, Traditional Techniquest for Healing the Soul.* Rochester, Vermont, USA: Destiny Books.

Desai, A. N. (2015, January 14). *albert-einstein-among-other-great-minds-proved-the-efficacy-of-micro-naps.* Retrieved from http://www.inquisitr.com: http://www.inquisitr.com/1754670/albert-einstein-among-other-great-minds-proved-the-efficacy-of-micro-naps/

Dumoulin, H. (2005). *Zen Buddhism: A History Japan* (Vol. 2 Japan). (J. W. Knitter, Trans.) Bloomington: World Wisdom, Inc. Retrieved 2008

Emoto, M. (2010, January 1). *Office Masaru Emoto.* Retrieved from www.masaru-emoto.net: http://www.masaru-emoto.net/english/water-crystal.html.

Happiness, L. (2017). Retrieved from Lotus Happiness: http://www.lotus-happiness.com/10-types-energy-healing-modalities/

Harris, H. (2010, January 1). *Ascension-Symptoms.* Retrieved from ascension 360: http://www.ascension360.net/resources-2/ascension-symptoms/

Harvard Health Publications. (2011, April). *Harvard Women's Health Watch.* Retrieved from In the journals: Mindfulness meditation practice changes the brain: https://www.health.harvard.edu/mind-and-mood/mindfulness-meditation-practice-changes-the-brain

Hawkins, D. R. (1995). Frequency Spectrum. In D. R. Hawkins, *Power vs. Force.* Sedona: Veritas Publishing.

Initiates, T. (1940). *The Kybalion A Study of The Hermetic Philosophy of Ancient Egypt and Greece.* (M. T. IL, Producer, & The Yogi Publication Society) Retrieved December 2016, from The Kybalion: http://www.kybalion.org/kybalion.php

KAMENETZ, A. (2011, May 18). *Meditate Your Way To A More Creative Mind.* Retrieved from Fast Company: https://www.fastcompany.com/1751573/meditate-your-way-more-creative-mind

Kennedy-Moore, E. (2013, January 31). *imaginary-friends.* Retrieved from psychologytoday.com: https://www.psychologytoday.com/blog/growing-friendships/201301/imaginary-friends

Labs, E. (1996). *Positive Ions versus Negative Ions.* Retrieved from Quantum Balancing: https://www.quantumbalancing.com/negative_ions.htm

Levine, P. (n.d.). *Classic Morita Therapy Consciousness, Zen, Justice and Trauma*. Retrieved from Books.Google: https://books.google.com/books?id=YpwuDwAAQBAJ&pg=PT168&lpg=PT168&dq=japan%27s+first+meditation+hall&source=bl&ots=_UGcsDVy25&sig=n893jBUz6XnWnaznWLyx20B2q3s&hl=en&sa=X&ved=0ahUKEwjljbmL4JDWAhUrxYMKHZCsB5gQ6AEIWzAL#v=onepage&q=japan's%20first%20meditation

Levy, G. (2012, January 13). *Thought Waves*. Retrieved from Frequencies: http://frequencies.ssrc.org/2012/01/13/thought-waves/

Lindgren, C. (2008). *Capturing the Aura, Integrating Science, Technology, and Metaphysics* (First Indian Edition ed.). (C. Lindgren, Ed.) Delhi, India: Motilal Banarsidass Publishers Private Limited. Retrieved 2016

Links, S. (2017). *Shaman Links*. Retrieved from Shaman Links: https://www.shamanlinks.net/shaman-info/about-shamanism/what-do-shamans-do/

MacMillan, A. (2017, June 16). *Yoga and Meditation Can Change Your Genes, Study Says*. Retrieved from Time.com: http://time.com/4822302/yoga-meditation-genes-stress/

MacMillan, A. (2017, January 05). *Yoga Is Officially Sweeping the Workplace.* Retrieved March 16, 2017, from TIME Health: http://time.com/4624276/yoga-workplace-mindfulness/

McKay, B. &. (2013, February 18). *Owning up to mistakes.* Retrieved from The art of Manliness: http://www.artofmanliness.com/2013/02/18/owning-up-to-mistakes/

Practice, S. f. (2017). *New to Shamanism?* Retrieved from Shamanic Practice: https://shamanicpractice.org/new-to-shamanism/

Press, O. U. (n.d.). *Oxford Dictionaries.* Retrieved from english Oxford Living Dictionaries: https://en.oxforddictionaries.com/definition/occult

Publications, A. H. (1997). *About Abraham Hicks.* Retrieved from Abraham-Hicks: http://www.abraham-hicks.com/lawofattractionsource/about_abraham.php

reiki7. (2016, November 21). Retrieved from medindia: http://www.medindia.net/alternativemedicine/reiki/reiki7.htm

Science, W. I. (1998, February 27). *ScienceDaily.* Retrieved from Science Daily: https://www.sciencedaily.com/releases/1998/02/980227055013.htm

Shamay, S. (2016, May 23). Editing Notes. (K. Shamay, Interviewer)

Sharma, N. (2016, July 25). *BioField Global Research Inc.* Retrieved from Biofield Global: http://www.biofieldglobal.org/what-is-human-aura.html

Stibal, V. (2016). *www.thetahealing.com.* Retrieved from Theta Healing spiritual, physical, emotional well being: http://www.thetahealing.com/about-thetahealing/thetahealing-theta-state.html

University of Bristol. (n.d.). *Alchemy.* Retrieved from University of Bristol School of Chemistry: http://www.chm.bris.ac.uk/webprojects2002/crabb/history.html

Unknown. (n.d.). Egyptian Tomb Art. *Unknown.* Egyptian National Museum, Online.

Vitale, J. &. (2007). *zerolimits.* Hoboken: John Wiley & Sons Inc.

Waikato, T. U. (2014, June 22). *Solids, liquids and gases.* Retrieved from Science Learning Hub: https://www.sciencelearn.org.nz/resources/607-solids-liquids-and-gases

Wikipedia. (n.d.). Retrieved from Wikipedia: https://en.wikipedia.org/wiki/Occult

Wilber, K. (2007, December 25). *Egolessness*. Retrieved from yogafly.blogs.com: http://yogafly.blogs.com/yogafly2/2007/12/egolessness-by.html

Wynne, A. (n.d.). *The Origin of Bhuddist Meditation*. New York: Routledge Taylor & Francis Group.

Keren Shamay

TAMT, EFTMP, METAP, Dr. Metaphysics

keren@kerenshamay.com

www.kerenshamay.com/energyworkcoaching

www.ingramcontent.com/pod-product-compliance
Lightning Source LLC
Chambersburg PA
CBHW070810100426
42742CB00012B/2316